Definitions from the Defined King James Bible

Extracted from the *DKJB* by Dr. Jung and his helpers in South Korea
With Additions and Enhancements by the original author of the definitions,
D. A. Waite, Jr. (M.A., M.L.A.)

4,114 Total Entries:

(294 Arc, 94 Obs, 32 Rare, 4 Poetic, 9 Dialec, 236 Gk, 86 Heb)

---

a testimony ~ i.e. an opportunity to testify or witness

a space ~ for a time

a ~ i.e. as a

abase ~ humble, humiliate; *Arc* lower, cast down

abased ~ humbled, humiliated; *Arc* lowered, cast down

abasing ~ humbling, humiliating; *Arc* lowering

abated ~ reduced in amount, degree, or force: diminished, weakened, deducted

abhor ~ hate, detest

abhorred ~ hated, detested

abhorrest ~ abhor: hate, detest

abhorreth ~ abhors ~ 5

abide after ~ remains according to

abide ~ remain, live, *Arc* stay; *Gk* wait for

abideth ~ abideth: remains, lives, continues as

abiding ~ remaining, continuing

abjects ~ miserable, wretched, degraded, lowly (ones)

abode ~ place where one lives or stays: home, residence, dwelling place

abode ~ past tense of abide: remained; stood fast; went on being; *Arc* stayed, resided (in or at)

abodest ~abode: past tense of abide: remained, stayed, dwelt

abomination ~ thing vile, disgusting, hateful, detestable, or loathsome

abominations ~ disgusting, hateful, detestable, loathsome things

abound ~ overflow abundantly

abounded ~ *Gk* overflowed, excelled

aboundeth ~abounds: overflows greatly

abounding ~ greatly or abundantly overflowing

abounds ~ overflows abundantly

about the space of ~ i.e. for about

about ~ all around; around

above that ~ beyond what

above ~ more than, beyond, over

above measure ~ i.e. beyond counting

abroad ~ i.e. widely

abroad ~ outside; far and wide; outdoors; *Gk* into view

abstinence ~ *Gk* abstinence from food

abundant ~ well-supplied, plentiful; great, rich

acceptation ~ agreement; *Arc* acceptance

acceptest ~ accept ~ 1

accepteth ~ accepts ~ 4

accomplished ~ completed

accord ~ in agreement, harmony; *Gk* one-minded; choice

accord ~ *Gk* united in spirit or harmonious

account ~ consider
account ~ an answer or explanation for conduct
accounted ~ counted, considered; credited
accounting ~ taking into account, considering
accursed ~ under a curse; deserving to be cursed; abominable
accuseth ~ accuses ~ 1
acknowledgeth ~ acknowledges ~ 1
acquaintance ~ persons known, but not intimately
activity ~ *Heb* ability, efficiency
adamant ~ in ancient times, a hard stone or substance that was supposedly unbreakable
addeth ~ adds ~ 4
addicted ~ devoted; dedicated
adjure ~ command or charge solemnly, often under oath or penalty
adjured ~ commanded or charged solemnly, often under oath or penalty
admiration ~ *Arc* astonishment, surprise, wonder
admired in ~ *Arc* marveled at by
admonish ~ warn, encourage
admonished ~ warned, encouraged
admonition ~ warning, mild rebuke, reproof
ado ~ trouble, fuss; uproar
adorn ~ embellish, decorate, beautify
adorned ~ decorated, beautified
adorneth ~ adorns: decorates, beautifies ~ 1
adorning ~ beautification, decoration
adria ~ the Adriatic sea
advantage ~ profit, usefulness
advantaged ~ profited, benefited

advantageth it me ~ i.e. profit or benefit is it to me
advantageth ~ advantages: profits, benefits ~ 1
adventure ~ venture, dare; *Obs* dare to go
adventured ~ risked
adversaries ~ opponents, enemies
adversary ~ enemy, opponent
advertise ~ tell, inform
advisement ~ careful consideration; counsel, advice
afar off ~ *Arc* at or from a distance; *Gk* from a distance
affairs ~ concerns
affect ~ seek, pursue, have affection for
affected ~ sought, pursued
affecteth ~ affects ~ 1
affinity ~ a relationship formed by marriage
affirm ~ firmly declare, confirm
afflict ~ mistreat
afflictest ~ afflict ~ 1
affording ~ furnishing, providing, giving, yielding
affright ~ *Arc* frighten, terrify
affrighted ~ *Arc* frightened, terrified
afoot ~ on foot
afore ~ *Dialect* before
afore ~ before
aforehand ~ beforehand
aforetime ~ *Arc* formerly, in times past
after ~ afterwards, in connection with (Gk); i.e. afterwards, later; *Gk* according to
against ~ in preparation for; until; by the time of; by the time that; opposite to; next to; *Arc* before; *Gk* in
agone ~ long before; *Arc* ago, past

agreeth ~ agrees: matches, harmonizes

ague ~ a fever, usually malarial, marked by regularly re-curring chills

ailed ~ troubled, bothered

aileth ~ ails: bothers, troubles, causes pain or distress

albeit ~ although, even though

algum ~ tree from Lebanon

alienated ~ made foreign, estranged, excluded

aliens ~ foreigners

all to brake ~ wholly or completely broke i.e. crushed

all hail ~*Arc* greetings; *Gk* rejoice

alleging ~ declaring

allow ~ acknowledge; *Gk* know

allow ~ approve, applaud; admit, accept

alloweth ~ allows: accepts, approves

allure ~ entice, tempt with a lure

almost ~ very nearly, but not completely; *Gk* with a little

alms ~ Money or goods given as charity to the poor; *Obs* deeds of mercy

almsdeeds ~ Money or goods given as charity to the poor; *Obs* deeds of mercy

aloof ~ at a distance

altereth ~alters: changes

altogether ~ entirely, totally

alway ~ *Arc* of always

amazed ~ *Obs* perplexed, alarmed, stunned

amazement ~ *Arc* fear-paralysis

ambassage ~ group of men sent out on a mission; a delegation

ambushment ~ ambush

ambushments ~ ambushes: persons hiding for attack

amend ~ improve; correct, emend, reform

amerce ~ punish by imposing an arbitrarily determined fine; punish generally

amiable ~ *Obs* lovely or lovable

amiss ~ in a wrong way, wrongly, improperly, astray

amongst ~ among

an hungred ~ hungry

an hundredfold ~ a hundred times as much

an help ~ i.e. a helper

an hand breadth ~ a hand's width

an advocate ~ one who pleads our case

an eight ~ eight

an hungred ~ hungry ~ 9

anathema ~ thing or person accursed or greatly detested

angle ~ hook and line used for fishing

anguish ~ great suffering, agony, distress, grief

anise ~ plant used for spice and medicine: dill

anointedst ~ anointed ~ 1

anointest ~ anoint ~ 1

anon ~ *Arc* immediately, at once

another ~ *Gk* another (of the same kind)

answer ~ reasoned defense; *Gk* apologia

answeredst ~ answered ~ 2

answerest ~ answer ~ 6

answereth ~answers: corresponds

answering again ~ talking back

any wise ~ any way

any while ~ i.e. for a long time

any ways ~ in any way or manner

apace ~ swiftly; with speed; at a fast pace

apart ~ aside

apothecaries ~ pharmacists or druggists
apothecaries' ~ pharmacists' or druggists'
apothecary ~ pharmacist or druggist
apparel ~ clothing, garments, attire;
apparelled ~ clothed, attired
appeareth ~ appears ~ 10
appeaseth ~ appeases ~ 1
appertain ~ pertain, relate, have to do with
appertained ~ pertained, related, had to do with
appertaineth ~ appertains: pertains, relates, has to do with
appertains ~ pertains, relates, has to do with
appointeth ~ appoints ~ 1
apprehended ~ *Obs* seize(d)
approacheth ~ approaches ~ 1
approvest ~ approve ~ 1
approveth ~ approves ~ 1
apt ~ *Arc* prepared, ready; *Gk* skillful
aquaintance ~ acquaintances
are asleep ~ i.e. are dead
aright ~ correctly, rightly; in a right way
ariseth ~ arises ~ 11
ark ~ box, chest, coffer
armholes ~ armpits or arm openings in a garment
armour ~ armor ~ 24
armourbearer ~ armorbearer ~ 18
armoury ~ armory ~ 3
arms ~ weapons; *Heb* forces
array ~ finery, apparel; military order or battle formation
arrayed ~ richly, royally, finely, lavishly dressed or clothed; dressed in fine, showy attire; decked out; dressed up
art mindful of ~ *Gk* remember

art ~ *Arc* are
artificer ~ skilled craftsman; inventor
artificers ~ skilled craftsmen; inventors
artillery ~ *Arc* apparatus for hurling missiles; bow & arrows
arts ~ i.e. magic or sorcery
as ~ seeing that, since, because; to the extent that
ascend ~ go (up)
ascended up ~ went up
ascended ~ went or gone up
ascendeth ~ goes up
ascendeth ~ ascends ~ 2
ascending ~ going up
ascribe ~ attribute, assign, impute; impute
askest ~ ask ~ 3
asketh ~ asks ~ 11
asp ~ any of several venomous African, Asian, or European snakes including some vipers and cobras
asps ~ any of several venomous African, Asian, or European snakes including some vipers and cobras
ass ~ donkey, burro
assay ~ attempt, try
assayed ~ attempted, tried
assaying ~ attempting, trying
assent ~ consent, agreement
assented ~ consented, agreed
asses ~ donkeys, burros
assuredly gathering ~ definitely concluding
assuredly ~ certainly, confidently
asswage ~ assuage--relieve; make less intense or severe
asswaged ~ old spelling of assuaged-- decreased, subsided, abated;

were made less intense or severe

astonied ~ *Obs* astonished: lit. "like a stone"

asunder ~ apart; into pieces or parts

at variance ~ put or place in conflict or disagreement; *Gk* cut into two parts, sever

at ~ near; to; i.e. out; i.e. in

at a venture ~ by mere chance, randomly

at enmity ~ having a strong, settled feeling of hatred

at even ~ *Arc* in the evening

at hand ~ i.e. near

at length ~ finally, after a long time

at strife ~ i.e. in conflict

at unawares ~ unintentionally, without knowing or being aware; unexpectedly, suddenly, by surprise

athirst ~ *Arc* thirsty

atonement ~ reconciliation; restoration to favor

attain to ~ reach

attained ~ achieved; arrived; *Gk* closely followed

attend upon ~ serve

attend ~ hear; *Arc* pay attention (to)

attendance ~ attention; service

attended to ~ *Arc* paid attention to, heard

attended ~ *Arc* paid attention

attending continually upon ~ *Gk* being steadfastly attentive unto

attent ~ attentive

augment ~ enlarge; increase

aul ~ *Arc* spelling of awl--pointed tool for making holes

austere ~ harsh, severe, or stern in look or manner

availeth ~ avails: has power to accomplish; is of use, help, or worth for; profits

avenge ~ inflict the Lord's deserved punishment; take revenge on behalf of

avenge not ~ do not take revenge on behalf of

avenge me of ~ inflict deserved, just punishment upon

avenged ~ inflicted punishment on behalf of

avenger ~ punisher

avengeth ~ avenges ~ 2

averse ~ turned away: unwilling, reluctant

avouched ~ openly acknowledged; asserted; affirmed

awakest ~ awake ~ 2

awaketh ~ awakes ~ 3

away with ~ tolerate, endure

axletrees ~ axles: shafts on which wheels rotate

babbler ~ producer of foolish, meaningless talk

backbiters ~ slanderers; those who speak maliciously about (an absent person)

backbiteth ~ backbites: slanders; speaks maliciously about (an absent person)

backbiting ~ slandering; speaking maliciously about (an absent person)

backbitings ~ slanderings; speakings maliciously about (an absent person)

bade ~ invited, asked, told; commanded (past tense of bid)

badest ~ bade> bid: told, asked, commanded

bag ~ money-bag

bakemeats ~ *Obs* pastries, pies; baked foods

baketh ~ bakes ~ 1

Balac ~ Balak ~ 1

balm ~ soothing ointment, salve

bands ~ things that bind, restraints: fetters, shackles, chains; *Heb* bonds; pangs; *Gk* ligaments

banquetings ~ carousings, drinking parties

baptizest ~ baptize ~ 1

baptizeth ~ baptizes ~ 2

barbarian ~ non-Greek, non-Roman; uncivilized, uncultured, crude, primitive

barbarians ~ non-Greeks, non-Romans; uncivilized, uncultured, crude, primitive ones

barbarous ~ non-Greek, non-Roman; uncivilized, uncultured, crude

bare ~ bore: carried, took up, lifted; gave; *Arc* of bore

barest ~ bear ~ 3

barked ~ stripped of all bark

barren ~ sterile, unable to conceive; empty

base ~ low(est), common, contemptible; *Obs* low or inferior in place or position

basest ~ lowest, most contemptible

bastard ~ illegitimate child

bastards ~ children born out of wedlock (illegitimately)

bath ~ Ancient *Heb* unit: 1 bath=6-10 gal

baths ~ Ancient *Heb* units: 1 bath=6-10 gal

battlement ~ parapet--a low protective wall or railing along the edge of a raised structure such as a roof or balcony

battlements ~ parapets--low protective walls or railings along the edge of a raised structure such as a roof or balcony

be no ~ are not

be mindful of ~ remember

be at charges ~ *Gk* incur expenses

bear long with them ~ puts up with them for a long time

bear ~ carry, sustain, support, lift; tolerate, put up with; *Gk* bear up under; endure; *Gk* wear, bear

bearest ~ bear ~ 5

beareth ~ bears: carries

bearing about ~ carrying around

bearing ~ carrying

beatest ~ beat ~ 2

beateth ~ beats ~ 1

became into ~ i.e. formed

became ~ was becoming to; was suitable or proper for

becamest ~ became ~ 2

beckoned ~ signaled; called or summoned by a silent gesture

beckoning ~ calling or summoning by a silent gesture as with a wave or nod; signaling

become ~ adorn: are right, fit, suitable, proper for

becometh us ~ is proper or fitting for us

becometh ~ becomes: suits, befits; adorns; is fitting to or proper for; is suitable to, worthy of, or appropriate for

bedstead ~ framework for supporting a mattress or bed

beeves ~ alternate plural of beef--a full-grown steer, bull, ox, or cow, especially one raised for meat

befall ~ happen (to)
befallen ~ happened (to)
befalleth ~ befalls: happens (to)
befell ~ happened or occurred (to)
beforetime ~ *Arc* formerly; at a time now past
begat ~ fathered, sired, procreated; produced
beget ~ father, sire, procreate; produce
begeteth ~ begets--fathers, sires, procreates; produces
begettest ~ beget: father, sire, procreate; produce
beggarly ~ inadequate; worthless; helpless; powerless
beginnest ~ begin ~ 1
begotten ~ fathered, sired, procreated; produced; generated
beguile ~ mislead or deprive by cheating or trickery; deceive; cheat, delude, trick
beguiled ~ deceived, cheated, deluded, tricked, misled
beguiling ~ deceiving, cheating, deluding, tricking, misleading
behaveth ~ behaves ~ 1
behaviour ~ behavior ~ 4
beheld ~ saw, observed, watched, looked at
behemoth ~ huge animal: perhaps an extinct dinosaur
behold ~ look at, see, observe, view closely, gaze upon; look upon; look! see!
beholdest ~behold: observe
beholdeth ~ beholds: looks at
beholding ~ seeing, watching
behoved ~ behooved: was necessary or proper for
being mindful of ~ remembering

belied ~ told lies about; misrepresented; contradicted; falsely portrayed
believest ~ believe ~ 8
believeth ~ believes ~ 45
belongest ~ belong ~ 1
belongeth ~ belongs ~ 20
bemoan ~ lament; mourn over; show grief or pity over
bemoaned ~ lamented; mourned over; showed grief or pity over
bemoaning ~ lamenting; mourning over; showing grief or pity over
bendeth ~ bends ~ 2
bent ~ determined, inclined
bereave ~ deprive or rob
bereaved ~ deprived, robbed
bereaveth ~ bereaves ~ 1
beseech ~ beg, entreat, implore; ask (someone) earnestly
beseeching ~ begging, entreating, imploring; asking earnestly
beset ~ encircle, surround; enclose; harass
beset ~ encircled, encompassed, surrounded; enclosed; harassed
beside ourselves ~ insane, crazy
beside ~ besides, in addition to
beside himself ~ insane, crazy
besieged ~ surrounded by an army (for a long time & cut off from supply)
besom ~ broom (made of twigs tied to a handle)
besought ~ begged, entreated, implored; asked (someone) earnestly
bestead ~ ill-treated, hard-pressed
bestir ~ stir-up, activate; rouse
bestow upon ~ give, present (as a gift or honor)

bestow ~ give, present, confer (as a gift or honor); *Arc* put, house, store

bestowed ~ given/gave, presented, conferred (as a gift or honor); *Arc* housed, put, stored, i.e. kept

bethink ~ *Arc* cause (oneself) to reflect on or consider remember; remind (oneself); recollect, recall

bethink themselves ~ *Arc* cause (oneself) to reflect on or consider remember; remind (oneself); recollect, recall

betimes ~ early, in good time; quickly; promptly, soon.

betrayest ~ betray ~ 1

betrayeth ~ betrays ~ 3

betroth ~ *Obs* promise to marry

betrothed ~ promised in marriage; engaged; *Obs* contracted to marry

bettered ~ improved, made better

betwixt ~ between, among

betwixt ~ between ~ 16

bewail ~ lament, mourn, wail over, express sorrow or unhappiness over

bewailed ~ lamented, mourned, wailed over; expressed sorrow or unhappiness over

bewaileth ~ bewails: laments, mourns, wails over; expresses sorrow or unhappiness over

bewitched ~ placed under his power by or as if by magic; cast a spell over; captivated completely; entranced

bewray ~ *Arc* divulge; reveal; betray

bewrayeth ~ bewrays: *Arc* divulges; reveals; betrays

bid you ~ i.e. tell you to

bid ~ ask, invite, tell; command; i.e. make

bidden ~ invited, asked, told (past tense of bid)

biddeth ~ bids: asks, invites, tells

bier ~ portable framework supporting a corpse or casket

bindeth ~ binds ~ 9

bishop ~ overseer

bishoprick ~ overseership; office or rank of an overseer

bishops ~ overseers

biteth ~ bites ~ 4

bittern ~ small bird similar to a heron

black ~ sad, dismal, gloomy; *Heb* dark, mournful

blackish ~ black-like

blains ~ skin swellings or sores; blisters; blotches; boils

blaspheme ~ speak of (God or a sacred entity) in an irreverent, impious manner; curse, revile; execrate

blasphemed ~ spoke(n) of (God or a sacred entity) in an irreverent, impious manner; cursed, reviled; execrated

blasphemer ~ one who speaks of (God or a sacred entity) in an irreverent, impious manner; one who curses, reviles, or execrates

blasphemers ~ ones who speak of (God or a sacred entity) in an irreverent, impious manner; ones who curse, revile, or execrate

blasphemest ~ speak irreverently, impiously

blasphemest ~ blaspheme ~ 1

blasphemeth ~ blasphemes: speaks of (God or a sacred entity) in an irreverent, impious manner; curses, reviles; execrates

blaspheming ~ cursing, reviling

blasting ~ any of several plant diseases of diverse causes, resulting in sudden death of buds, flowers, foliage, or young fruits; the withering caused by atmospheric conditions

blaze ~ proclaim, publish

blemish ~ deformity

blessest ~ bless ~ 3

blesseth ~ blesses ~ 8

blindeth ~ blinds ~ 1

blotted out ~ erased

blotteth ~ blots ~ 1

bloweth ~ blows ~ 4

blueness ~ Heb: bruise, stripe

boastest ~ boast ~ 1

boasteth ~ boasts ~ 4

boisterous ~ rough and stormy, turbulent

bolled ~ budded; (boll=roundish seed pod of a plant)

bolster ~ pillow, cushion; *Heb* head place

bond ~ bond-slave; *Gk* doulos

bond ~ band, fetter, shackle; i.e. bondage

bond ~ contract, covenant, binding agreement; a duty or agreement by which one is bound; a promise

bondmaid ~ slave-girl

bondmaids ~ slavegirls

bondman ~ slave (male)

bondmen ~ slaves (male)

bonds ~ bands, chains, fetters, shackles

bondservant ~ slave

bondservice ~ slavery

bondwoman ~ slave (female)

bondwomen ~ slaves (female)

bonnets ~ caps

booties ~ plunder

booty ~ plunder, loot

borne of ~ carried by

borne ~ tolerated, put up with; carried, taken, lifted up; *Gk* worn, born

borrow ~ ask

borrowed ~ asked

borroweth ~ borrows ~ 1

bosom ~ chest; i.e. robe-covered chest area

bosses ~ knobs or projections protruding from a flat surface

botch ~ boil, ulcer, tumor, or other eruptive disease; swelling, pimple, sore,

bound ~ compelled, obliged

bound ~ boundary, limit

bounds ~ boundaries, limits

bountifully ~ generously

bountifulness ~ generosity

bounty ~ generosity; gift freely given

bow ~ i.e. rainbow

bowels ~ interior of anything, esp. the body: guts, intestines, innards; *Arc* the seat of pity or the gentler emotions: fig. compassionate feelings or tender emotions

boweth ~ bows ~ 3

bowing ~ curved, crooked

box ~ *Heb* vial, flask

box ~ evergreen like the boxwood

brakest ~ break> broke ~ 5

bramble ~ prickly, thorny shrub

brand ~ stick that is burning

brasen ~ brazen: like brass in color or other qualities; brass=a yellowish metal essentially an

alloy of copper and zinc: from
an OE word meaning brass or
bronze; *Heb* copper or bronze
(a copper alloy)

bray ~ crush or pound into powder, as
in a mortar; pulverize

bray ~ make the loud, harsh cry of a
donkey

brayed ~ made the loud, harsh cry of
a donkey

breach of promise ~ breaking of
promise; *Heb* opposition

breach ~ break, crack, gap, broken
place; breaking, bursting forth,
outburst (of anger)

breaches ~ breaks, cracks, gaps,
broken places or parts

breakest ~ break> broke ~ 1

breaketh ~ breaks ~ 17

breatheth ~ breathes ~ 1

breeches ~ garments that cover the
breech or buttocks i.e.
undergarments; trousers
reaching to the knees

brethren ~ brothers

brickkiln ~ kiln (or furnace) for
drying bricks

bridleth ~ bridles ~ 1

brigandine ~ armor; originally armor
for a brigand (irregular
soldier, robber, bandit)

brigandines ~ armor (plural);
originally armor for a brigand
(irregular soldier, robber,
bandit)

brimstone ~ lit burn-stone--sulfur:
burns with a blue flame &
stifling odor, used in making
black gun powder

bring forward on ~ *Gk* provide the
necessities for

bringest ~ bring ~ 5

bringeth ~ brings ~ 79

brink ~ edge, bank

broided ~ braided, interwoven

broidered ~ embroidered, adorned
with needlework

broughtest ~ brought ~ 13

bruit ~ *Arc* rumor, report, sound,
noise; news; fame

brutish ~ beast-like: stupid, irrational;
brutal, cruel; crude,
uncivilized

buckler ~ small round shield held by
a grip or worn on the arm; any
protection or defense

bucklers ~ small, round arm-shields

buffet ~ strike with the fist or hand;
punch, slap

buffeted ~ struck with the hand or
fist: slapped; punched

buildedst ~ builded> ~ built ~ 1

buildeth ~ builds ~ 9

bullock ~ young bull, steer; male
cattle raised for beef

bullocks ~ young bulls, steers; male
cattle raised for beef

bulrush ~ marshland plant like the
cattail or papyrus

bulrushes ~ marshland plants like the
cattail or papyrus

bulwarks ~ defensive walls,
earthworks

bunches ~ *Obs* humps

burneth ~ burns ~ 18

burnished ~ polished

busybodies ~ gossips, meddlers

busybody ~ gossip, meddler

butlership ~ office of butler

buyest ~ buy ~ 2

buyeth ~ buys ~ 3

by the space of ~ i.e. for; *Obs* for

by reason of ~ i.e. because; *Gk*
through

by ~ in; nearby; *Gk* through

by an equality ~ out of fairness
by and by ~ immediately, at once
by occasion of ~ through
by reason ~ i.e. because
byword ~ object of scorn, ridicule, reproach or derision
calamities ~ great or deep troubles or miseries; disasters
calamity ~ great or deep trouble or misery; disaster
caldron ~ large kettle
caldrons ~ large kettles
call over ~ *Gk* name upon
calledst ~ called ~ 4
callest ~ call ~ 3
calleth ~ calls ~ 30
calve ~ give birth to a calf
calved ~ gave birth to a calf
calveth ~ calves: gives birth to a calf
camest ~ came ~ 28
can skill ~ *Obs* has/have skill
canker ~ anything that corrupts or gradually decays; gangrene, malignant growth, ulcer; rust; from L cancer
cankered ~ rusted, corrupted, decayed, eaten away
cankerworm ~ any of several larvae of geometrid moths harmful to fruit and shade trees, esp the spring cankerworm that feeds on fruit and foliage
canst ~ can ~ 51
carbuncle ~ *Arc* any of certain deep-red gems
carbuncles ~ *Arc* any of certain deep-red gems
care of ~ concern for
care ~ concern, anxiety, or worry
care ~ be concerned, worried, or anxious

careful ~ full of care, worry, or concern: anxious, worried, concerned
carefulness ~ anxiety, worry, concern
careless ~ worry-free; securely, safely
carelessly ~ in a worry-free manner
cares ~ worries, anxieties, concerns
carest ~ care ~ 3
careth ~ cares ~ 7
carnal ~ material; *Gk* fleshly
carnally ~ i.e. sexually
carriage ~ that which is carried: luggage, baggage
carriages ~ things that are carried: luggage, baggage
carriest ~ carry ~ 1
carrieth ~ carries ~ 3
carry tales ~ slander
cast lots ~ randomly make decisions using objects
cast out ~ *Gk* exposed
cast the same in his teeth ~ likewise taunted or mocked
cast their young ~ i.e. miscarried
cast their young ~ i.e. miscarry
cast up ~ construct by digging
cast forth ~ thrown out
cast clouts ~ cast-off or discarded pieces of cloth or rag often used as patches
cast angle ~ fish with a hook and line
cast a mount ~ build (*Obs*) a raised fortification
cast ~ *Gk* revolved , turned over
cast ~ threw; Brit vomited
cast ~ threw
cast ~ throw, fling, or hurl (with force or violence); drive; throw, i.e. spit
cast ~ thrown
cast ~ build, construct; form by pouring into mold

castaway ~ reject, discard
castedst ~ casted> ~ cast ~ 1
castest ~ cast ~ 3
casteth not her calf ~ delivers not her young prematurely
casteth ~ casts: throws, drops
casting up mounts ~ building (*Obs*) raised fortifications
casting ~ mold
casting ~ throwing, putting
catcheth ~ catches ~ 3
caul ~ membrane or fatty tissue surrounding an organ
cauls ~ close fitting caps or nets worn by women
causest ~ cause ~ 2
causeth ~ causes ~ 32
causeway ~ paved road, highway
cease to pray ~ i.e. stop begging, imploring, or beseeching
cease ~ stop
ceased to kiss ~ i.e. stopped kissing
ceased ~ stopped
ceaseth ~ ceases ~ 10
ceasing of ~ stopping by
ceasing ~ stopping; intermission
celestial ~ heavenly; pertaining to the sky or heavens; of heavenly origin or nature
censer ~ container in which incense is burned (a shortened form of ME encenser)
centurion ~ Roman commander of 100 soldiers
centurions ~ Roman commanders each in charge of 100 men
certain ~ certain (ones)
certain ~ fixed, definite
certified ~ assured, informed (with certainty)
certify ~ inform (with certainty); *Arc* assure

chafed ~ irritated, annoyed
challengeth ~ challenges ~ 1
chamber ~ room
chambering ~ *Arc* sexual indulgence or lewdness
chamberlain ~ originally, the bedchamber attendant of a ruler or lord; later, a ruler or lord's household manager, steward; *Heb* official, eunuch
chamberlains ~ originally, the bedchamber attendants of a ruler or lord; later, a ruler or lord's household managers, stewards; *Heb* officials, eunuchs
chambers ~ rooms
chamois ~ small mountain goat-antelope having straight horns with tips bent backwards; a soft leather made from the skin of such an animal
champaign ~ broad plain; flat, open country
chance ~ happen to be
chanceth ~ chances ~ 1
changest ~ change ~ 1
changeth ~ changes ~ 2
chapiter ~ top part (head or capital) of a column, pillar, or pilaster
chapiters ~ top parts (heads or capitals) of a column, pillar, or pilaster
chapmen ~ *Arc* peddlers, traders, merchants; men whose business is buying and selling
chapt ~ chapt=chapped: cracked open, split; roughened
charge ~ responsibility, duty; custody, care, supervision
charge ~ command, warn
charge ~ command, warning
chargeable ~ burdensome, a burden

charged ~ warned, commanded, ordered; entrusted; burdened

chargedst ~ charged ~ 1

charger ~ *Arc* platter; large, flat dish; something that carries a load (from charge: to load)

chargers ~ *Arc* platters; large, flat dishes; things that carry a load (from charge: to load)

charges ~ duties, responsibilities; expense

chargest ~ charge ~ 1

charging ~ warning, comanding

charitably ~ in a manner consistent with unselfish concern

charity ~ the love of God for humanity, or a love of one's fellow human beings; an act of goodwill or affection; the feeling of goodwill, benevolence; kindness or leniency in judging others; a voluntary giving of money or other help to those in need; money or help so given; an institution or other recipient of such help (In the KJV charity is always a translation of the Greek word agapA, a word that suggests unselfish, self-sacrificing concern.)

chaseth ~ chases ~ 1

chasten ~ correct by punishing: correct, punish

chastened ~ punished, beaten

chastenest ~ chasten ~ 1

chasteneth ~ chastens: correctively punishes: severely rebukes with words & chastises with blows

chastise ~ punish by beating

chastiseth ~ chastises ~ 1

check ~ any sudden stop or repulse (from the game of chess); *Obs* reproof, reprimand, rebuke, censure; *Heb* discipline, correction, chastening

cheereth ~ cheers ~ 1

cherisheth ~ cherishes ~ 2

cheweth ~ chews ~ 8

chide ~ loudly or passionately express anger, dissatisfaction, disappointment, disagreement, or discouragement: argue, quarrel, complain

chiding ~ loudly or passionately expressing anger, dissatisfaction, disappointment, disagreement, or discouragement: arguing, quarreling, complaining, contending

chief rooms ~ most important places (at table)

chief ~ *Gk* presidents

chief ~ main; greatest; i.e. leaders

chiefest ~ *Gk* first in rank or honor

chiefly ~ especially; mainly

chode ~ loudly or passionately expressed anger, dissatisfaction, disappointment, disagreement, or discouragement: argued, quarreled, complained

choler ~ anger, wrath, irascibility, ill-humor (Latin for bile, thought to be the source of anger and irritability)

choosest ~ choose ~ 2

chooseth ~ chooses ~ 3

church ~ assembly

churl ~ rude, coarse, surly, ill-bred person; boor; selfish or mean person; villain; *Heb* scoundrel, knave

churlish ~ rude, coarse, surly, ill-bred; boorish; selfish or mean; villainous; *Heb* hard, cruel, severe, stubborn

cieled ~ ceiled: covered or lined with plaster or thin boards (used of a room's ceiling or walls); *Heb* wainscoted, paneled

circuit ~ going around; circular path; orbit; i.e. a regular, circular route

circumspect ~ cautious, wary, careful; considerate; discreet, prudent; careful to consider all circumstances before acting, judging, or deciding;

circumspectly ~ cautiously, warily, carefully; considerately; discreetly, prudently; carefully considering all circumstances before acting, judging, or deciding;

cistern ~ container for catching rain-water

clamour ~ clamor: *Gk* loud demand or complaint

clappeth ~ claps ~ 1

clave ~ clung

clave ~ split

clean ~ completely

cleanseth ~ cleanses ~ 3

clear ~ pure, clean

clear ~ acquit; free; excuse

clearing of yourselves ~ defense

clearing ~ acquitting

cleave ~ cling

cleave ~ split, divide

cleaved ~ clung

cleaveth ~ cleaves: clings

cleaveth ~ cleaves: splits

cleft ~ split

clemency ~ mercy, mildness

clift ~ hole, crevice

clifts ~ older form of clefts: spaces made by cleaving (splitting); *Heb* chasms, ravines, steep slopes; clefts

climbeth ~ climbs ~ 1

cloke of covetousness ~ disguise or pretense of greed

cloke ~ cloak: veil or cover

close ~ shut-up: quiet

closest ~ close ~ 1

closet ~ small private room for reading, meditation, etc.

clothest ~ clothe ~ 1

clouted ~ patched

cloven ~ split, divided

clovenfooted ~ with a split or divided foot or hoof

coast ~ border, region, country

coasts ~ borders, regions, countries

cock crew ~ rooster crowed

cock ~ rooster

cockatrice ~ a fabulous serpent supposedly hatched from a cock's (rooster's) egg and having power to kill by a look; *Heb* poisonous snake; viper or adder (from OFr cocatris--crocodile)

cockle ~ any of various weeds that grow in grain fields: darnel, tares, weeds; *Heb* stinkweed

coffer ~ chest, box, trunk, or coffin

cogitations ~ thoughts, reflections, considerations, or meditations

college ~ building used for worship or education; educational or religious building

collops ~ folds of fatty flesh on the body

colour ~ color ~ 14

coloured ~ colored ~ 1

colours ~ colors ~ 12

come by ~ control, secure

comeliness ~ *Heb* ornament, splendor, majesty; honor, glory; *Gk* charm or excellence of figure, external beauty, decorum, modesty, seemliness

comely ~ beautiful, pretty, fair, pleasing; appropriate, fitting, becoming; *Arc* seemly, decorous, proper

comest ~ come ~ 29

cometh ~ comes ~ 282

comfortedst ~ comforted ~ 1

comforteth ~ comforts ~ 5

commandedst ~ commanded ~ 4

commandest ~ command ~ 3

commandeth ~ commands ~ 13

commend ~ entrust; recommend; *Gk* demonstrate, display, exhibit

commended of ~ praised by

commended ~ entrusted

commendeth ~commends: recommends; praises; demonstrates, displays

commending ~ recommending

commit sacrilege ~ rob temples i.e. plunder pagan shrines

committest ~ commit ~ 1

committeth ~ commits ~ 19

commodious ~ suitable, convenient

commotions ~ *Arc* civil uprisings

commune ~ converse, i.e. communicate, talk, speak

communed ~ conversed; i.e. communicated, talked, spoke

communicate ~ impart, give, share, confer; convey knowledge, information, or something tangible; *Gk* fellowship, become a partaker together

communicated ~ imparted, gave, shared, conferred; conveyed knowledge, information, or something tangible; *Gk* fellowshiped, became a partaker together

communication ~ sharing; *Gk* fellowship

communications ~ *Gk* words: conversations; *Gk* companionships, communion (homilia)

companied ~ *Arc* associated

company ~ *Arc* associate

compass thee round ~ *Arc* surround, circle; encompass thee

compass ~ *Arc* circled, went around; took a detour

compass ~ *Arc* circle; go around; encompass; surround

compass ~ *Arc* circumference, enclosed area or space, width (*Heb* edge, rim)

compassed ~ *Arc* encircled, enclosed; encompassed; surrounded; went/gone around

compassed about ~ *Arc* encircled, enclosed; surrounded; went around

compassest ~ compass: *Arc* encircle, enclose; surround; go around

compasseth ~ compasses: *Arc* encircles, encloses; surrounds; goes around

compassing ~ *Arc* encircling, enclosing; surrounding

compellest ~ force

compellest ~ compel ~ 1

compoundeth ~ compounds ~ 1

comprehended ~ understood, mentally grasped; included, comprised; *Gk* summarized

concealeth ~ conceals ~ 2

conceit ~ opinion

conceits ~ opinions

concerneth ~ concerns ~ 2

concision ~ cutting off or mutilation; division or schism

concluded ~ *Gk* enclosed

concord ~ agreement, harmony; (from root "same heart/ mind"); *Gk* concord, agreement: sumphonAsis

concourse ~ assembly of people, crowd, throng, gathering; a large open area or hall where a crowd gathers; (from root meaning "running together")

concubine ~ secondary wife--inferior socially and legally

concubines ~ secondary wives-- inferior socially and legally

concupiscence ~ strong desire or appetite, esp. sexual desire-- lust; lasciviousness, eroticism, lechery

condemned ~ punished, fined

condemnest ~ condemn ~ 1

condemneth ~ condemns: slights, scorns, despises, or treats with contempt

condescend to ~ descend voluntarily to the level of

conduct him forth ~ *Obs* escort him

conducted ~ lead, guided

conduit ~ pipe or channel for carrying fluid

coney ~ small, rabbit-like nocturnal animal that lives in rock holes; perhaps a hyrax

confection ~ something mixed together; a concoction; *Heb* a spice mixture

confectionaries ~ ones who mix things together; concoction makers; *Heb* ointment-makers, perfumers, spice-mixers

confederacy ~ union, alliance; people or group united for some common purpose

confederate ~ united, allied

confesseth ~ confesses ~ 3

confirmeth ~ confirms ~ 3

confound ~ confuse, perplex; *Arc* destroy

confounded ~ confused, perplexed; ashamed, disgraced; bewildered

congealed ~ thickened, coagulated, jelled

conies ~ small, rabbit-like nocturnal animals that live in rock holes; perhaps hyraxes

consecrated ~ set apart as holy

consentedst ~ consented ~ 1

considerest ~ consider ~ 2

considereth ~ considers ~ 9

consist ~ *Arc* hold together

consisteth ~ consists ~ 1

consolation ~ comfort

consorted ~ associated, kept company

constantly ~ continually

constrain ~ compel, force, oblige, or strongly encourage

constrained ~ compelled, forced, obliged, or strongly encouraged

constraineth ~ constrains: compels, forces, obliges, or strongly encourages

constraint ~ compulsion, force, obligation

consulteth ~ consults ~ 1

consumeth ~ consumes ~ 4

consumption ~ wasting away of the body; a disease that causes this, esp tuberculosis of the lungs; destruction

contain ~ exercise self-control

containeth ~ contains ~ 1

contemn ~ slight, scorn disdain, despise, or treat with contempt

contemned ~ scorned, disdained, despised, treated with contempt

contemneth ~ contemns ~ 1

contemptible ~ utterly despised or scorned

contemptuously ~ scornfully

contend ~ dispute, debate, fight

contended ~ disputed, argued, fought

contendest ~ contend: dispute

contendeth ~ contends ~ 3

contention ~ discord, conflict, dispute, strife; controversy, quarrel

contention ~ struggle

contention ~

contentions ~ conflicts, disputes, quarrels

contentious ~ always ready to argue; quarrelsome

continueth ~ continues ~ 5

contradiction ~ opposition

contrariwise ~ on the other hand, on the contrary

contrary ~ opposed, antagonistic; unfavorable; opposite

convenient ~ appropriate, suitable fitting

conversant among ~ familiar or acquainted with

conversant ~ acquainted

conversation ~ behavior, conduct, manner of life; *Gk* citizenship, commonwealth

converted ~ changed, transformed

converteth ~ converts ~ 1

conveyed ~ transported, taken

convince ~ prove guilty, vanquish, refute

convinced ~ proved guilty, vanquished, refuted

convinceth ~ convicts, proves guilty

convinceth ~ convinces ~ 1

convocation ~ group called together; assembly, gathering

coping ~ top layer of masonry wall

coppersmith ~ artisan who makes or repairs copper objects, esp by shaping the metal while it is hot and soft

cormorant ~ large voracious sea bird

corn ~ grain (various types); kernel

cornet ~ small horn

cornets ~ small horns

cornfloor ~ grain floor; *Heb* threshing floor, barn floor

correcteth ~ corrects ~ 2

corrupt ~ debase; deceitfully peddle

corrupt ~ *Gk* corrupted & unfit for use; rotten

corrupteth ~ corrupts ~ 1

corruptible ~ perishable

costliness ~ abundance of costly things

cotes ~ small shelters or sheds for fowl, sheep, doves, etc

couch ~ crouch or lie down

couch ~ (portable) bed or couch: i.e. cot

couched ~ crouched or lay down

coucheth ~ couches ~ 1

couchingplace ~ resting place

could skill of ~ *Obs* have skill with

couldest ~ could ~ 5

coulter ~ alt of colter: vertical iron blade in front of plow

coulters ~ alt spell of colters: iron blades in front of a plow that make a vertical cut in the soil

council ~ advisers (of a Roman official); *Gk* Great Council or Sanhedrin

councils ~ assemblies of judges

counsel ~ purpose, will; *Arc* intention, resolution, purpose

counsel ~ advise

counsellor ~ counselor: advisor; *Gk* member of the Sanhedrin; senator

count ~ consider, think, account

counted ~ considered

countenance ~ i.e. facial expression: attitude; i.e. favor

countervail ~ counteract, counterbalance; compensate for; equal in value; match

counteth ~ counts ~ 3

coupled ~ joined

coupleth ~ couples: joins

course ~ way, path; i.e. turn; opportunity to run, flow, or move; i.e. organizational unit, division

courses ~ i.e. organizational divisions; shifts

covenant ~ treaty; binding, solemn agreement

covenanted ~ solemnly agreed

coveredst ~ covered ~ 2

coverest ~ cover ~ 2

covereth ~ covers ~ 27

covert ~ covered or protected place; shelter or hiding place

covet ~ ardently want; long for with envy; earnestly desire

coveted after ~ greedily longed for

coveted ~ enviously longed for

coveteth ~ covets ~ 2

covetous ~ greedy (one[s])

covetous ~ greedy, grasping

covetousness ~ insatiable (unsatisfied) desire for more; greed

cracknels ~ light, crisp biscuits

craft ~ trade

craft ~ guile; slyness; deception, trickery

craveth ~ craves ~ 1

createth ~ creates ~ 1

creature ~ created (thing); creation

creditor ~ one to whom a debt is owed

creepeth ~ creeps ~ 14

crew ~ crowed

crib ~ rack, trough, or box for fodder; manger

criest ~ cry ~ 5

crieth ~ cries ~ 17

crime laid against him ~ *Gk* accusation

crisping pins ~ curling pins for the hair

crookbackt ~ crook backed; hunch-backed; hump-backed

crop ~ sacklike enlargement of a bird's gullet where food

croucheth ~ crouches ~ 1

crownedst ~ crowned ~ 1

crownest ~ crown ~ 1

crowneth ~ crowns ~ 1

cruse ~ small vessel for liquids

cry ~ outcry, shout

cubit ~ c. 18 to 22 inches

cubits ~ each cubit= c. 18 to 22 inches

cuckow ~ *Heb* meaning unknown; possibly an extinct bird; perhaps a seagull

cumbered ~ encumbered, overwhelmed, troubled, burdened

cumbereth ~ cumbers: encumbers, burdens, hinders, obstructs

cumbrance ~ troublesome burden, encumbrance, hindrance

cummin ~ plant with bitter, warm-tasting seeds

cunning ~ Adj--skillful, clever; sly, crafty;

cunning ~ Noun--skill; craftiness, slyness

cunningly ~ cleverly

curious ~ carefully, intricately, or skillfully made; highly detailed or elaborate in workmanship

cursedst ~ cursed ~ 2

cursest ~ curse ~ 1

curseth ~ curses ~ 10

custom ~ tribute, tax, toll

cuttest ~ cut ~ 1

cutteth ~ cuts ~ 6

dainties ~ choice foods, delicacies

dainty ~ delicious, choice; delicately pretty or lovely

dale ~ valley

dam ~ mother of an animal; mother (variant of dame--lady)

damnation ~ condemnation; doom; consignment to eternal punishment (from Fr damn--condemn); *Gk* judgment

damned ~ condemned; doomed; consigned to eternal punishment (from Fr damn--condemn)

damsel ~ girl, maiden

damsels ~ girls, maidens

dandled ~ danced up and down

darkeneth ~ darkens ~ 1

darling ~ beloved; favorite; one and only (from O.E. deorling: "dearling" diminutive of dear)

dart ~ pointed missile: dart, arrow, javelin

darts ~ sharp-pointed weapons: arrows, spears

dash ~ smash

dasheth ~ dashes ~ 2

daub ~ cover, coat, or plaster with any substance

daubed ~ covered, coated, or plastered with any substance

daubing ~ coating, plaster

daysman ~ mediator, arbiter, umpire

dayspring ~ daybreak, sun-rising, early dawn

deal ~ portion, share, part, allotment

deal ~ distribute

dealest ~ deal ~ 2

dealeth ~ deals ~ 10

deals ~ portions, parts

dearth ~ drought, famine (lack or scarcity of anything, esp food)

debase ~ reduce in value, quality, dignity, rank or position

decayeth ~ decays ~ 3

decease ~ death

deceased ~ died

deceivableness ~ deceit, deception, deceitfulness

deceiveth ~ deceives ~ 6

deck ~ adorn, decorate; cover, clothe (with finery or ornaments)

decked ~ adorned, decorated; covered, clothed (with finery or ornaments)

deckedst ~ decked: adorned, decorated; covered, clothed (with finery or ornaments)

deckest ~ deck: adorn, decorate; cover, clothe (with finery or ornaments)

decketh ~ decks: adorns, decorates; covers, clothes (with finery or ornaments)

declare ~ explain, interpret

declareth ~ declares ~ 4

decline ~ deviate, diverge, turn away from, fall away from

declined ~ deviated, diverged, turned from, fallen from

declineth ~ declines: deviates, diverges, turns from, falls from

deep ~ Poetic: the sea or the ocean

defendest ~ defend ~ 1

defer ~ delay, postpone

deferred ~ postponed, delayed, put off

deferreth ~ defers: delays

defiledst ~ defiled ~ 1

defileth ~ defiles ~ 9

defraud ~ take away, deprive, or withhold property, rights, etc. by fraud; cheat, rob

defrauded ~ taken away, deprived, or withheld property or rights by fraud

degree ~ step, status, or standing

delayeth ~ delays ~ 2

delectable ~ delightful, pleasing, delicious

deliciously ~ luxuriously, sensually, wantonly

delightest ~ delight ~ 1

delighteth ~ delights ~ 14

delightsome ~ delightful, pleasurable, enjoyable

deliveredst ~ delivered ~ 3

deliverest ~ deliver ~ 2

delivereth ~ delivers ~ 13

delusion ~ false belief

demanded of ~ i.e. interrogated in a demanding way by

denieth ~ denies ~ 4

denounce ~ *Obs* announce, esp in a menacing way

departed asunder ~ went apart; *Gk* separated

departed ~ *Obs* divided in two

departeth ~ departs ~ 8

deputed ~ appointed, assigned, authorized

deride ~ ridicule, scorn, mock, make fun of

derided ~ ridiculed, scorned, mocked, made fun of

derision ~ ridicule, scorn, contempt; object of ridicule, scorn, contempt

descend ~ come or go down

descended ~ went or came down

descendeth ~ descends ~ 1

descending ~ going or coming down

descent ~ downward slope

describe ~ divide, delineate, trace the form or outline of

described ~ divided, delineated, outlined, traced

describeth ~ describes ~ 2

description ~ division, delineation, outline

descry ~ observe; spy out, put under surveillance; search out

desert ~ deserted, uninhabited

deserts ~ deserted or uninhabited (places)

deserveth ~ deserves ~ 1

desired to tarry ~ encouraged to stay

desired ~ summoned or called for; asked; i.e. asked a

desiredst ~ desired ~ 2

desirest ~ desire ~ 2

desireth ~ desires ~ 17

desirous of vain glory ~ eager for empty praise

desolate ~ uninhabited, deserted; barren, lifeless, alone

desolation ~ devastation, ruin

despise dominion ~ view authority with contempt

despise ~ scorn, hate, detest; look down upon with contempt or scorn

despised ~ hated, scorned, detested; looked down on with contempt; disregarded, rejected

despisers of ~ haters that look down upon

despisest thou ~ *Gk* do you think little or nothing of

despisest ~ despise ~ 1

despiseth ~ despises: looks down on with contempt & scorn; disregards; *Gk* rejects, refuses

despite ~ *Arc* contempt, scorn, spitefulness

despiteful ~ *Arc* spiteful, malicious

despitefully ~ *Arc* spitefully, maliciously

destitute ~ completely lacking, devoid, empty, poverty-stricken; *Obs* abandoned, forsaken

destroyest ~ destroy ~ 4

destroyeth ~ destroys ~ 8

determinate ~ settled, decided; conclusive

devices ~ plans: evil schemes or tricks

devil ~ demon, evil spirt; *Gk* diabolis slanderer, devil: metaphorical (one devil, many demons)

devilish ~ demon-like

devils ~ demons, evil spirits; (*Heb* hairy ones; satyrs)

deviseth ~ devises ~ 8

devotions ~ *Gk* objects of worship, i.e. idols, altars, temples

devourest ~ devour ~ 1

devoureth ~ devours ~ 10

diadem ~ royal crown; crown-like ornamental headband

dial ~ i.e. sun-dial

did very abominably ~ acted in a very vile, loathsome, detestable, disgusting, or hateful manner

diddest ~ did ~ 1

didst ~ did ~ 122

diest ~ die ~ 1

dieth ~ dies ~ 30

differeth ~ differs ~ 2

diggedst ~ digged, ~ dug ~ 1

diggeth ~ digs ~ 3

dignities ~ *Arc* dignitaries: persons holding a high, dignified position

dined ~ eaten dinner

dippeth ~ dips ~ 2

directeth ~ directs ~ 3

dirt ~ excrement

disallow ~ refuses to allows; rejects as untrue, invalid

disallowed ~ disapproved; rejected, repudiated

disannul ~ completely cancel, annul, nullify

disannuleth ~ disannuls: completely cancels, annuls, nullifies

disannulled ~ completely canceled, annulled, nullified

disannulling ~ complete canceling, annulling, nullifying

disappointeth ~ disappoints ~ 1

discerned ~ examined, discerned; recognized

discerneth ~ discerns ~ 1

discharged ~ unloaded

discomfited ~ *Arc* defeated, routed, put to flight; destroyed

discomfiture ~ *Arc* defeat, rout

discord ~ lack of harmony, dissension, conflict

discover ~ *Arc* reveal, expose, uncover

discovered ~ *Arc* uncovered, displayed, exposed, revealed; *Arc* sighted

discovereth ~ discovers: *Arc* uncovers, displays, exposes, reveals

disguiseth ~ disguises ~ 1

dishonour ~ dishonor ~ 11

dishonourest ~ dishonor ~ 1

dishonoureth ~ dishonors ~ 3

dismayed ~ afraid, troubled; alarmed

disorderly ~ in a lawless, unruly, disorderly way

dispensation ~ stewardship, economy, administration, management

dispersed abroad ~ distributed widely

dispersed ~ scattered

disposed ~ inclined, willing

disposition ~ arrangement, means

disputation ~ discussion; debate; dispute, argument, quarrel

disputations ~ discussions; debates; disputes, arguments

disputed ~ debated, argued

disputer ~ debater

disputing ~ *Gk* discussion, disputation

disputings ~ arguments

disquiet ~ disturb, distress, trouble; make anxious, uneasy, restless

disquieted ~ distressed, troubled; made anxious, restless

disquietness ~ distress; anxiety, restlessness

dissembled ~ disguised or concealed real nature, motives, or feelings behind a false appearance; behaved hypocritically

dissemblers ~ hypocrites; pretenders

dissembleth ~ dissembles: acts hypocritically; disguises or conceals real nature, motives, feelings behind a false appearance

dissension ~ strife, violent wrangling; violent quarreling; i.e. riot

dissimulation ~ hypocrisy, duplicity, deception

dissolvest ~ dissolve ~ 1

dissolving ~ ending

distaff ~ staff on which fibers, as flax, wool or tow, are wound before being spun into thread

distil ~ fall in drops, trickle, drip

distress ~ necessity or distress

distributeth ~ distributes ~ 1

divers ~ different, various, several (ones) ·

diverse ~ different

diversities ~ differences

divideth ~ divides ~ 10

divination ~ prediction by magic; the act or practice of trying to foretell the future or explore the unknown by occult means

divine ~ foretell the future by occult means; prophesy (through occult means)

divine divinations ~ prophesy by occult means

diviners ~ foretellers of the future or the unknown by occult means

divineth ~ practices divination, foretells the future

divineth ~ divines ~ 1

divining ~ foretelling future by occult means

divorcement ~ divorce

do iniquity ~ *Gk* practice lawlessness

do err ~ do wrong, deviate from the right

do ~ i.e. want

doctors ~ teachers or learned men

doest ~ do ~ 45

doeth ~ does ~ 96

doleful ~ sorrowful, mournful, gloomy

dominion ~ sovereign authority, power, or rule; lordship

dominions ~ sovereign lordships

done ~ i.e. finished

dost ~ do ~ 56

dote ~ say, think, or do foolishly; become foolish

doted ~ had a foolish or excessive affection or lust

doth ~ does ~ 207

doting ~ having a foolish or excessive fondness

doubletongued ~ deceitful or insincere in speech

doubted of ~ was uncertain about

doubteth ~ doubts ~ 1

doubtless ~ without a doubt; at least, truly, indeed

downsitting ~ sitting down

dowry ~ money paid to wife as divorce security; gift, endowment; *Arc* gift from a man to his bride

drag ~ dragnet

dragon ~ *Obs* Bible a word used to translate one Hebrew word meaning dragon or dinosaur; sea or river monster; or serpent or venomous snake

dragons ~ *Obs* Bible a word used to translate one Hebrew word (15x) meaning dragons or dinosaurs; sea or river monsters; or serpents or venomous snakes A second Hebrew word is rendered dragon only in Mal 3:1. It's

meaning is uncertain: dragons, jackals, sea monsters (??)

drams ~ lit. handful, then a weight or coin, and finally a measure; weight today=1/16 oz (about 5/16 oz in Bible times)

draught ~ Brit spell for draft: a drawing in of a fish net; the amount of fish caught in one draw

draught ~ privy, toilet, sewer

drave ~ drove: drove (*Arc* spelling)

draw ~ drag

drawers ~ haulers

draweth ~ draws ~ 12

dreameth ~ dreams ~ 2

dress ~ prepare: clean and eviscerate (an animal)

dressed ~ prepared: cleaned and eviscerated (for eating); cultivated

dresser ~ caretaker

dresseth ~ dresses: prepares (for use); trims

drew ~ dragged

drewest ~ drew ~ 1

driedst ~ dried ~ 1

drieth ~ dries ~ 3

drinketh ~ drinks ~ 17

driveth ~ drives ~ 4

dromedaries ~ one-humped Arabian camels, esp ones trained for fast riding

dromedary ~ one-humped Arabian camel, esp one trained for fast riding

droppeth ~ drops ~ 1

drove ~ animals moving as a group: flock, herd

dryshod ~ with dry shoes

due season ~ proper time; *Gk* our own time

due ~ proper; *Gk* his own

due benevolence ~ required
      "kindness" i.e. conjugal duty
dues ~ debts
duke ~ chief, leader, noble
dukes ~ chiefs, leaders, noblemen
dulcimer ~ *Heb* meaning uncertain:
      stringed instrument or any
      instrument making a pleasant
      sound [?]
dumb ~ voiceless, mute
dung ~ refuse, waste matter; manure,
      excrement; or anything
      morally filthy
dung ~ fertilize with dung, manure,
      refuse
dunghill ~ heap or pile of refuse,
      waste matter, manure,
      excrement
dunghills ~ heaps or piles of refuse,
      waste matter, manure,
      excrement
dureth ~ *Arc* form of endures: lasts,
      continues, persists
dureth ~ dures>endures ~ 1
durst ~ dares to; dared
durst ~ dare ~ 9
dwell ~ live
dwellest ~ live
dwellest ~ dwell ~ 19
dwelleth ~ dwells: lives
dwelt ~ lived
ear ~ plow [*Arc*]
ear ~ grain or seed bearing spike of
      cereal plant, esp corn
eared ~ tilled, plowed
earing ~ plowing or plowing time
      [*Arc*]
early ~ in the near future; *Heb* early,
      earnestly, diligently
earnest ~ down payment: money paid
      in advance as part payment to
      bind a contract or bargain;

promise or assurance: a token
      of something to come
earneth ~ earns ~ 2
earthen vessels ~ clay containers
Easter ~ Ishtar--ancient pagan
      festival: from ME ester
      (spring) and Eastre (dawn
      goddess); Easter was
      originally the name of a pagan
      spring festival that occurred at
      about the same time as the
      Passover. *Gk* passover
easy to be intreated ~ *Gk* compliant
eatest ~ eat ~ 3
eateth ~ eats ~ 56
edification ~ building up
edified ~ built up
edifieth ~ edifies: builds up
edify not ~ don't build up
edify ~ build up (morally or
      spiritually)
edifying ~ building up
effect ~ accomplish
effect ~ result (*Heb* service, labor,
      work)
effect ~ "maketh . . . Of none
      effect"=frustrates, restrains
effect ~ "spake . . . To that [effect]"=
      spoke . . .about this
effect ~ accomplishment, result; i.e.
      fulfillment
effect ~ force, influence, or power
effect ~ "made . . . Of none effect" =
      nullified, canceled
effect ~ "making . . . Of none effect"=
      nullifying
effectual ~ effective; fully adequate
effectually ~ effectively; fully
      adequately
effeminate ~*Gk* lit: soft, soft to the
      touch; fig (in a bad sense):
      effeminate--of a catamite (a

boy sexually used by an adult pedophile); of a boy kept for homosexual relations with a man; of a male who submits his body to unnatural lewdness; of a male prostitute

elders ~ *Gk* presbuterion: body of elders, senate

elect ~ chosen (ones)

elect's ~ chosen one's

elected ~ chosen

election ~ choice, choosing, selection

elements ~ elementary principles, basics

Elias ~ Elijah ~ 30

else ~ otherwise

emboldened ~ made bold or bolder; given courage, encouraged

emboldeneth ~ emboldens: makes bold; gives courage, encourages, incites

emerods ~ *Arc* related to hemorrhoids=blood+flow; *Heb* tumors, hemorrhoids; (ulcers??)

eminent ~ high, lofty; towering, prominent

emulation ~ desire or ambition to equal or surpass; *Obs* ambitious rivalry, envious dislike

encampeth ~ encamps ~ 2

enchantment ~ magic spells, or charms

endamage ~ inflict damage upon; injure; discredit

endeavour ~ endeavor ~ 1

endeavoured ~ endeavored: tried

endeavouring ~ endeavoring: striving, trying

endeavours ~ endeavors ~ 1

endeth ~ ends ~ 1

endow ~ pay the required dowry price for

endued ~ supplied, provided, endowed; Rare: clothed

endureth ~ endures ~ 59

engines ~ machines, instruments; apparatuses

engrafted ~ implanted; firmly established or planted

engraven ~ carved, engraved

enjoin ~ urge or impose with authority and emphasis: command, order

enjoined ~ urged or imposed with authority and emphasis: commanded, ordered

enlarged ~ magnified

enlargement ~ *Arc* release from confinement or bondage (*Heb* relief)

enlargeth ~ enlarges ~ 3

enmity ~ hostility, strong hatred

enquirest ~ enquire, ~ inquire ~ 1

enrichest ~ enrich ~ 1

ensample ~ *Arc* of example: sample, pattern, model

ensamples ~ *Arc* of examples: samples, patterns, models

ensign ~ flag, banner, or standard, esp a military one raised high as a rallying point for troops

ensigns ~ flags, banners, or standards, esp a military ones raised high as a rallying point for troops

ensue ~ *Arc* pursue, follow, strive for

entangleth ~ entangles ~ 1

entereth ~ enters ~ 20

enterprise ~ an undertaking or project, esp a difficult, bold, dan-gerous, or important one

enticeth ~ entices ~ 1

enticing ~ pleasing, alluring

entreat ~ *Arc* treat, behave toward

entreated ~ *Arc* treated; behaved toward

entreateth ~ entreats ~ 1

enviest ~ envy ~ 1

envieth ~ envies ~ 1

environ ~ surround, encircle, encompass

ephah ~ ancient Hebrew unit of dry measure estimated at from 1/3 bu to 1+ bu (8 gal or 36L)

ephod ~ richly embroidered outer vestment worn by Jewish priests; shoulder cape; mantle

epistle ~ letter, esp a long, formal, instructive one

epistles ~ letters, esp long, formal, instructive ones

equality ~ fairness, equity, equality

equity ~ fairness, impartiality, justice

ere ~ *Arc* before, until

err ~ do wrong, swerve, deviate, or wander from what is right; fall into error; go astray; commit an error

errand ~ purpose or object for being sent: mission, message

erred ~ swerved, gone astray; done wrong

erreth ~ errs ~ 2

Esaias ~ Isaiah

escapeth ~ escapes ~ 6

eschew ~ avoid; shun; abstain from; keep away from

eschewed ~ avoided; shunned; abstained from; kept from

escheweth ~ eschews: avoids; shuns; abstains from; keeps away from

espied ~ spied, caught sight of; watched; saw

espousals ~ betrothals, engagements; weddings

espoused ~ betrothed, engaged, promised in marriage; taken as a spouse, especially as a wife; married

espy ~ spy, catch sight of; see

establisheth ~ establishes ~ 3

estate ~ state, status, condition; place, office; property, possessions

estates ~ i.e. nobles

esteem other ~ consider or value the other

esteem ~ *Obs* value

esteemed ~ valued, respected

esteemeth ~ esteems ~ 4

esteeming ~ considering, valuing

estranged ~ made foreign, removed, alienated; separated; kept away

eunuch ~ (castrated or emasculated) male employed as a chamberlain or high officer by an Oriental potentate

even ~ *Arc* evening

eveningtide ~ *Arc* evening

eventide ~ *Arc* evening

ever a lover ~ always a friend

ever ~ forever; always

ever ~ ere: before

evermore ~ emphatic synonym of ever: always, continually

evident token ~ clear sign, plain proof

evident ~ clear, plain

evidently ~ clearly, plainly

evil eye ~ green-eyed jealousy or bewitching stare

evil affected ~ negatively influenced

evil ~ i.e. diseased

evilfavoredness ~ {*Arc*} deformity, ugliness; (*Heb* injury)

ewe ~ female sheep

ewes ~ female sheep

exact usury ~ require at (excessively high) interest

exact ~ force payment, practice extortion; require, demand

exacted ~ required or forced payment of

exacteth ~ exacts ~ 1

exactions ~ forced payments; extortions

exactors ~ {*Arc*} taskmasters; (oppressors; extortioners)

exaltest ~ exalt ~ 1

exalteth ~ exalts ~ 9

examination had ~ *Gk* completing a preliminary investigation

examined of ~ questioned or interrogated about

examined ~ interrogated, questioned

exceedest ~ exceed ~ 1

exceedeth ~ exceeds ~ 1

exceeding ~ *Arc* of exceedingly: extremely, surpassing, very; *Arc* very great

exceedingly ~ extremely, beyond measure, to a great degree; greatly, loudly

exceedingly the **more** ~ extremely more

excellency ~ excellence; superiority; *Gk* elevation, pre-eminence, superiority

excellent ~ *Gk* majestic

excellest ~ excel ~ 1

excelleth ~ excels ~ 3

except ~ *Arc* unless, i.e. if; but;

exchangers ~ *Obs* money chargers, exchange brokers, bankers (*Gk* those who exchange money for a fee and pay interest on deposits)

execration ~ curse

execute ~ carry out, perform

executed ~ carried out, performed

executed ~ performed, carried out

executedst ~ executed ~ 1

executest ~ execute ~ 1

executeth ~ executes ~ 6

executing ~ performing, carrying out, doing

exercised thereby ~ trained by it

exerciseth ~ exercises ~ 1

exhort ~ urge, strongly encourage; warn

exhortation ~ encouragement, warning

exhorted ~ encouraged, warned

exhorteth ~ exhorts ~ 1

exhorting ~ urgently instructing, or warning

expecting ~ expectantly waiting

expedient ~ advantageous, profitable; needful; useful or suited for the purpose or situation

expelled ~ threw or forced (out)

experiment ~ trial, test

expired ~ ended

expounded ~ explained, interpreted

extendeth ~ extends ~ 1

extol ~ praise highly

extolled ~ praised

extortioner ~ one using threats or force to get money

extortioners ~ ones using threats or force to get money

eyeservice ~ service done only while the master sees; work done only in master's sight

fadeth ~ fades ~ 7

faileth ~ fails: is lacking or deficient

fain ~ *Arc* willingly, gladly, with eagerness

faint not ~ *Arc* don't lose courage, strength, or hope

faint ~ *Arc* lose strength, courage or hope

faintest ~ faint ~ 1

fainteth ~ faints ~ 4

fair ~ lovely, attractive, beautiful, good-looking

fairs ~ markets, bazaars: scheduled gatherings of people for bartering, trading, or selling goods

fall not out ~ don't quarrel, argue, or fight

fallen asleep ~ i.e. dead

fallest ~ fall ~ 1

falleth out ~ occurs, arises

falleth ~ falls: i.e. belongs

fallow deer ~ a small Eurasian deer (Dama dama) having a yellowish-red coat spotted with white in summer and broad, flattened antlers in the male

fallowdeer ~ fallow deer: a small Eurasian deer (Dama dama) having a yellowish-red coat spotted with white in summer and broad, flattened antlers in the male

fame abroad ~ rumor or report far & wide

fame ~ *Arc* public report, rumor

familiar spirits ~ demons supposed to be in association with or under the power of a man

familiar spirit ~ demon supposed to be in association with or under the power of a man

fan ~ winnow grain with a fork-like instrument; scatter with a fork-like winnowing instrument

fan ~ fork-like instrument for winnowing

fanners ~ scatterers, winnowers

far spent ~ i.e. almost over

fare ye well ~ *Gk* prosper: farewell (letters)

fare ~ do

fared sumptuously ~ feasted magnificently

farthing ~ lit. "little fourth"; an old British coin worth a fourth of a penny; thing of little value; small piece of anything

farthings ~ lit. "little fourths"; old British coins worth a fourth of a penny

fashion ~ manner: bearing, actions, way of life

fashioneth ~ fashions ~ 3

fashioning ~ patterning, conforming

fast ~ specifically: the Day of Atonement

fast ~ *Obs* close, near

fast ~ abstain from food (entirely or partially) as a religious observance or a sign of grief

fast ~ firm

fast ~ firmly, fixedly; firmly fastened; firmly to; rapidly

fasted ~ abstained from food

fastest ~ fast ~ 1

fasting ~ abstaining from food; with no food

fastings ~ food-deprivations, starvations

fat ~ i.e. choicest, best part; abundance (of produce); i.e. thick, healthy, stout, robust; fig. the best, good

fat ones ~ *Heb* fatlings

fat ~ i.e. prosperous; i.e. rich, plentiful, abundant; i.e. fruitful, fertile; *Heb* vigorous, stalwart ones

fat ~ i.e. richly prepared food

fatfleshed ~ fat + fleshed: fat, plump; fatter

fathers ~ forefathers

fathoms ~ one fathom is c. 6 feet

fatling ~ calf, lamb, kid, or young pig fattened for slaughter

fatlings ~ calves, lambs, kids, or young pigs fattened for slaughter

fatness ~ i.e. plenty, prosperity; i.e. choice or best portions

fats ~ *Arc* vessels of large size for liquids: tubs; dyers or brewers vats; wine casks (*Heb* wine vats, wine-presses)

fattest ~ i.e. best, choicest

fault ~ *Gk* falling beside or near; lapse or deviation from truth or righteousness; misdeed; sin

favour ~ favor ~ 70

favourable ~ favorable ~ 4

favoured ~ favored ~ 14

favourest ~ favour, ~ favor ~ 1

favoureth ~ favours, ~ favors ~ 1

fearest ~ fear ~ 3

feareth ~ fears ~ 20

feeble ~ weak

feebleminded ~ *Arc* faint-hearted

feedest ~ feed ~ 2

feedeth ~ feeds ~ 8

feign ~ pretend; disguise or conceal; act or allege falsely

feigned ~ pretended; deceitful, counterfeit; hypocritical

feignedly ~ deceptively, falsely, hypocritically

feignest ~ *Arc* feign: pretend; fabricate, make-up

fell on sleep ~ fell asleep: i.e. died

fell asleep ~ i.e. died

fell a lusting ~ i.e. began to lust

fell ~ i.e. chop down

felled ~ i.e. chopped down

feller ~ lumberjack, tree-chopper

fellest ~ fell ~ 1

felling ~ chopping down

felloes ~ the curved pieces of wood which, joined together, form the circular rim of a spoked wheel; exterior rims of spoked wheels (alt fellies)

fellows ~ associates, companions, partners

fenced ~ defenced, i.e. walled

fens ~ swamps, marshes, bogs; wetlands

fervent mind ~ zeal

fervent ~ burning: zealous, ardent; intensely devoted or earnest

fervently ~ intensely, earnestly

fetch a compass ~ *Arc* circle or go around; take a circular course

fetch ~ bring; get; retrieve

fetched a compass of ~ *Arc* circled or went around; made a detour for

fetched ~ brought, retrieved, got(ten)

fetcheth ~ fetches: brings i.e. makes

fetcht ~ fetched: brought, retrieved, got

fetters ~ shackles, metal bands, or chains for the feet (or hands)

fidelity ~ faithfulness

fighteth ~ fights ~ 3

figure ~ figure of speech, type, metaphor, emblem; *Gk* parable

figures ~ *Gk* anti-types

filledst ~ filled ~ 2

fillest ~ fill ~ 1

fillet ~ flat square molding separating other moldings; narrow band between two grooves in a column

filleted ~ ornamented with encircling bands

filleth ~ fills ~ 6

fillets ~ flat square moldings separating other moldings; narrow bands between two grooves or flutings in a column

filthy lucre ~ illicit, dishonorable, or unlawful gain or advantage

findest ~ find ~ 2

findeth ~ finds ~ 27

fine ~ shortened form of refine: refine, purify

finer ~ refiner, smelter, silver (or gold) smith

fining ~ refining (fining pot=crucible)

firebrands ~ pieces of burning wood

firkins ~ lit "fourths": each firkin=1/4 barrel--a little less than 9 English gallons

firmament ~ sky, viewed poetically as a solid arch or vault; the vault or expanse of the heavens

firstbegotten ~ first-born; first-fathered

firstling ~ firstborn, first of a kind

firstlings ~ firstborn ones, first ones of a kind

fitches ~ vetches: vicia sativa (or nigella sativa) plants or just the small, black acrid seeds used as a seasoning; *Heb* black cumin

fitly ~ properly, suitably

fitted to ~ suited, adapted, prepared for

fitteth ~ fits ~ 1

fixed ~ un-movable, firmly fixed; established, steadfast; steady

flag ~ marshland plant: reed, rush, cattail, iris

flagon ~ *Heb* raisin-cake, used in sacrificial feasts

flagons ~ earthen or skin containers; jugs, jars; skin-bags

flagons ~ "flagons of wine"=raisin-cakes of grapes (used in sacrificial feasts) cf Heb

flags ~ marshland plants: reeds, rushes, cattails, irises

flanks ~ fleshy sides of an animal between the last rib and the hips: sides

flattereth ~ flatters ~ 6

flay ~ strip off the skin or hide of, as by whipping; skin

flayed ~ stripped off skin or hide of, as by whipping; skinned

fleddest ~ fled ~ 2

fleeth ~ flees ~ 8

fleshhook ~ hook for flesh; large fork

fleshhooks ~ hooks for flesh; large forks

flieth ~ flies ~ 5

flight ~ fleeing

floats ~ rafts

flourished ~ vigorously grown, thrived

flourisheth ~ flourishes ~ 2

flowers ~ *Arc* menstrual flow

floweth ~ flows ~ 12

fluttereth ~ flutters ~ 1

flux ~ any excessive or unnatural discharge of fluid body matter, esp from the bowels ("bloody flux"=*Gk* dusenteria: dysentery, bowel ailment)

foameth ~ foams ~ 2

foes ~ enemies

fold ~ times

foldeth ~ folds ~ 1

followedst ~ followed ~ 1

followeth ~ follows ~ 15

foot ~ i.e. base

footmen ~ *Arc* men who go on foot such as foot soldiers

for to ~ i.e. in order to; i.e. to; *Arc* unless

for to sojourn ~ in order to stay, dwell, or live temporarily

for that ~ instead; i.e. because; *Gk* because

for ~ because of

for all ~ i.e. although

forasmuch ~ for+as+much: since, because; inasmuch (as)

forbad ~ forbade ~ 5

forbare ~ *Arc* for forbore: ceased, stopped

forbear to help ~ refrain from helping; avoid helping

forbear ~ refrain (from), abstain (from); cease, stop, avoid; restrain; endure, tolerate

forbearance ~ toleration, patience; self-restraint

forbeareth ~ forbears: *Arc* ceases, forgoes; rejects: i.e. fails

forbearing ~ refraining from (*Gk* omitting, giving up)

forbearing ~ i.e. restraining myself, holding it in; *Gk* sustaining, holding up; enduring

forbiddeth ~ forbids ~ 1

forborn ~ ceased, hesitated

forecast ~ arrange, plan, scheme, or contrive

forefront ~ front-most part, extreme front

foreknew ~ knew before

foreknowledge ~ forethought; *Gk* foreknowledge, pre-arrangement

foremost ~ first, farthest to the front

foreordained ~ ordained or appointed beforehand

forepart ~ front part

foreseeth ~ foresees ~ 2

foreship ~ ship's bow or forward part

forgat ~ forgot ~ 8

forgavest ~ forgave ~ 2

forgettest ~ forget ~ 2

forgetteth ~ forgets ~ 4

forgiveth ~ forgives ~ 2

formeth ~ forms ~ 2

fornication ~ legally: sexual relations between unmarried persons; *Gk* any kind of illicit sexual relations

fornicator ~ *Gk* male prostitute

fornicators ~ practicers of sexual sin

forsaketh ~ forsakes ~ 6

forsomuch as ~ i.e. since, because

forsookest ~ forsook ~ 2

forswear thyself ~ renounce an oath; swear falsely, perjure thyself

forth ~ out, forward

forthwith ~ immediately, at once, without delay

forum ~ marketplace

forward ~ willing

forwardness ~ zeal, eagerness; inclination, readiness

foul ~ evil; stormy

fouledst ~ fouled ~ 1

founder ~ one who founds or casts metal or glass in a mold

foundest ~ found ~ 1

fourfold ~ four times as much; four times, i.e. with four lambs

fourscore ~ eighty (a score is 20)

foursquare ~ adj: with four equal sides; n: *Arc* square

fowl ~ flying creature(s): bird(s), flying insect(s)

fowler ~ bird-hunter

fowlers ~ bird-hunters

fowls ~ flying creatures: birds, winged insects

fragments ~ food-remnants: i.e. leftovers

frame ~ form, framework, structure

frame ~ manage; form; conform

frameth mischief ~ brings about harm, injury, damage

frameth ~ frames ~ 2

frankincense ~ aromatic gum resin burned as a fragrant incense

frankly ~ *Gk* freely, graciously

fray ~ *Arc* frighten, scare, terrify (afraid=affrayed)

fret ~ eaten away, decayed

fret ~ eat away, gnaw; irritate, vex; annoy; worry

fretted ~ worried, irritated

fretteth ~ frets: is being angry, vexed, irritated

fretting ~ eating, gnawing, or corroding

frontlets ~ things worn on the forehead: phylacteries--small leather cases holding slips inscribed with Scripture

froward ~ stubbornly willful; not easily controlled; contrary; twisted; perverted: disposed to go contrary to the reasonable or required

frowardly ~ in a stubbornly willful way

frowardness ~ stubborn willfulness; perversity; disposition to go contrary to the reasonable or required

frustrateth ~ frustrates ~

full ~ fully

fuller ~ lit. bleacher: one who fulls cloth--cleans and whitens it by stamping or beating it in a chemical solution

furbish ~ polish, brighten, brush, or clean

furbished ~ polished, brightened, brushed, or cleaned

furious ~ wildly raging, violently angry

furlongs ~ lit. long furrow: the length of a furrow in common field of 10 acres; a furlong is 1/8 of an English mile--c.200 yards

furniture ~ anything furnished or provided: furnishings, equipment, supplies (*Heb* basket saddle)

furtherance ~ advancement, progress

gaddest ~ gad: move about restlessly, roam idly

gainsay ~ speak against, contradict, oppose, hinder

gainsayers ~ speakers against, contradictors, opponents, hinderers

gainsaying ~ speaking against, contradicting, opposing, hindering; "bad-mouthing"

gall ~ something bitter or distasteful; bile; *Arc* gall-bladder

gallant ~ stately, imposing; beautiful in appearance

garlands ~ wreaths of flowers

garner ~ storehouse for grain; granary; grain-bin

garners ~ granary, place for storing grain; grain-bins

garnish ~ decorate, embellish, adorn

garnished ~ decorated, embellished, adorned

gat ~ got

gatherest ~ gather ~ 1

gathereth ~ gathers ~ 17

gave him audience ~ listened to him

gave place ~ yielded

gave suck ~ nursed

gave ear ~ listened, paid attention

gave audience ~ *Obs* gave a hearing; *Gk* listened

gavest ~ gave ~ 34

gay ~ fine (*Gk* shining, splendid, magnificent)

gazingstock ~ object of someone's stare; a spectacle; i.e. object of public humiliation

gender ~ *Arc* of engender: breed, generate, produce

gendered ~ *Arc* of engendered: bred, generated, produced

gendereth ~ genders: *Arc* of engenders--breeds, generates, produces, reproduces

generation of vipers ~ descendants of poisonous snakes

getteth ~ gets ~ 9

ghost ~ spirit

gier eagle ~ a bird of prey; maybe a kind of carrion vulture; perhaps an extinct bird; exact meaning unknown

gin ~ short for engine: mechanical device, trap, or snare

gins ~ engines: mechanical devices, traps, or snares

gird ~ encircle, fasten, or secure with a belt or band; clothe

girded ~ encircled, fastened, or secured with a belt or band; clothed

girdedst ~girded: encircled, fastened, or secured with a belt or band; clothed

girdeth ~ girds: encircles, fastens, or secures with a belt or band; clothes

girding ~ wrapping, binding

girdle ~ belt or sash worn around the waist

girdles ~ belts or sashes worn around the waist

girt ~ encircled, fastened, or secured with a belt or band

give in charge ~ *Gk* command

give my child suck ~ nurse my child

give place ~ make room: i.e. leave, withdraw; provide a place or opportunity

give suck ~ nurse

give thee charge ~ command you

give ear ~ listen, pay attention

give audience ~ *Gk* listen

given ~ addicted, inclined; *Gk* enslaved

givest ~ give ~ 12

giveth ~ gives ~ 126

giving out ~ making public; *Gk* saying

glad tidings ~ happy news

glass ~ mirror

glasses ~ mirrors

glean it ~ collect what has dropped

glean ~ collect the leavings from (the harvesting process); gather the produce left behind by the harvesters; gather what reapers drop

gleaned ~ gathered

gleanings ~ leavings, leftovers: dropped by harvesters

glede ~ lit =glide: bird of prey like a buzzard, kite, or hawk

glistering ~ shinning, sparkling, glittering (glister=*Arc* of glitter)

gloriest ~ glory ~ 1

glorieth ~ glories: boast(s)

glorifieth ~ glorifies ~ 1

glory of ~ rejoice in

glory ~ rejoice, boast

glorying of ~ boasting about

glorying ~ boasting

gluttonous ~ greedy for food; excessively over-eating

gnash ~ grind or chew (in anger or pain)

gnashed ~ ground or chewed (in anger or pain)

gnasheth **upon** **him** **with** **his** **teeth** ~ grinds his teeth at him (in anger)

gnasheth ~ gnashes: grinds or chews (in pain or fear)

gnashing ~ grinding (in pain or anger)

go **to** ~ *Arc* come, come on; indeed

go **a** **whoring** ~ prostitute themselves: lit. through cult prostitution to false gods or fig. by spiritual unfaithfulness to the true God

god **speed** ~ good success i.e. God bless you

godhead ~ Godhood, divinity, deity

gods ~ *Heb* elohim i.e. judges

goest ~ go ~ 46

goeth ~ goes ~ 135

going ~ departure (*Heb* marching, anklet)

goldsmith ~ artisan who makes or repairs gold objects, esp by shaping the metal while it is hot and soft

goldsmiths ~ artisans who make or repair gold objects, esp by shaping the metal while it is hot and soft

gone **a** **whoring** ~ prostituted themselves: lit. through cult prostitution to false gods or fig. by spiritual unfaithfulness to the true God

goodly ~ good-looking; good-quality, fine; good-sized

goodman ~ male head of household; host; husband

gopher ~ meaning and exact type unknown: cypress wood ?

governor ~ helmsman

graffed ~ grafted

grave ~ dignified, serious; sober, serious, important; somber

grave ~ engrave, carve (*Arc* of engrave)

graven ~ metal, melted and cast into a mold

graven ~ carved, sculptured; engraved

graveth ~ graves: carves

graving ~ engraving, carving (*Arc* of engraving)

gravity ~ solemnity or sedateness of manner or character; earnestness; dignity, seriousness

greater **part** ~ majority

greaves ~ leg-armor that covers from ankle to knee

Grecia ~ Latin for Greece

Grecians ~ Greek-speaking Jews

greeteth ~ greets ~ 1

greyhound ~ perhaps an extinct animal

grieveth ~ grieves ~ 2

grievous ~ burdensome, heavy; severe, harsh; painful; very serious; grief-producing; causing pain or grief; *Gk* cruel

grievously ~ severely, harshly, painfully

grievousness ~ harshness, severity

grisled ~ gray-colored (whole or spotted); variant of grizzled-- grizzle

groaneth ~ groans ~ 1

gropeth ~ gropes ~ 1

gross ~ thick, dense; fat, corpulent, heavy (Fr thick)

ground ~ *Obs* foundation, solid base
groweth ~ grows ~ 14
grudge ~ grumble; begrudge, be
     envious; harbor hostility; ill
     will; *Gk* sigh, groan
grudging ~ muttering, complaining;
     resentment
grudgingly ~ reluctantly
guile ~ deceit, deception, cunning,
     craftiness, trickery
gulf ~ wide, deep chasm or abyss
habergeon ~ sleeveless coat, jacket or
     poncho of protective armor
     that is shorter than a hauberk
     (*Heb* corselet: a piece of
     armor formerly worn to
     protect the trunk)
habergeons ~ sleeveless coats, jackets
     or ponchos of protective
     armor that is shorter than a
     hauberk (*Heb* corselets--
     pieces of armor formerly worn
     to protect the trunk)
habitation ~ home, dwelling place
habitations ~ dwellings; settlements
had ~ held
had in abomination with ~ viewed as
     disgusting, detestable, or
     loathsome
had in remembrance ~ remembered
had indignation ~ i.e. were angry
hadst ~ had ~ 22
haft ~ handle, hilt (that which is held)
hale ~ *Arc* draw, haul; pull with force
     or violence
haling ~ *Arc* drawing, hauling; pulling
     with force or violence
hallow ~ make holy, consecrate,
     sanctify, set apart
hallowed ~ made holy, consecrated,
     sanctified, set apart

hallowed ~ holy, consecrated,
     sanctified, set apart, purified
halt ~ *Arc* lame, crippled
halt ~ *Arc* walk with a crippled gait;
     limp; hobble
halted ~ *Arc* walked with a crippled
     gait; limped; hobbled
halteth ~ *Arc* walks with a crippled
     gait; limps; hobbles
halteth ~ halts, ~ limps ~ 2
halting ~ *Arc* walking with a crippled
     gait; limping; hobbling
handleth ~ handles ~ 3
handmaid ~ *Arc* handmaiden: female
     servant or attendant
handmaiden ~ *Arc* female servant or
     attendant
handmaidens ~ *Arc* female servants
     or attendants
handmaids ~ *Arc* handmaidens:
     female servants or attendants
handstaves ~ *Arc* staffs carried as a
     weapon: i.e. war clubs
hangeth ~ hangs ~ 2
hap ~ *Arc* chance; luck; lot
haply ~ by chance; *Arc* by chance or
     accident; perhaps
happeneth ~ happens ~ 6
hard ~ *Arc* close, near
hard by ~ *Arc* close by, near to
hardeneth ~ hardens ~ 4
hardly ~ *Rare* with difficulty or
     effort; harshly, severely
hardness ~ hardships
harlot ~ prostitute (originally a
     euphemism for whore)
harlots ~ prostitutes (originally a
     euphemism for whores)
harness ~ *Arc* armor (or other military
     equipment)
harnessed ~ armed for battle; in battle
     array

harrow ~ draw or drag a harrow over (harrow=a frame with spikes or sharp-edged disks, drawn by a horse or tractor and used for breaking up and leveling plowed ground, covering seeds, rooting up weeds

harrows ~ frames with spikes/sharp-edged disks, drawn by a horse or tractor and used for breaking up/leveling plowed ground, covering seeds, rooting up weeds

hart ~ male deer (esp a male red deer of five years), stag

harts ~ male deer (esp a male red deer of five years), stags

hast ~ has ~ 1071

haste ~ hurry

hasted ~ hurried

hasten ~ hurry

hastened ~ hurried

hasteneth ~ hastens ~ 1

hasteth ~ hastes: hurries

hasting ~ hurrying

hatcheth ~ hatches ~ 1

hatest ~ hate ~ 6

hateth ~ hates ~ 31

hath ~ has ~ 2263

haunt ~ frequent; visit often

haunt ~ place often visited or much frequented

have ~ *Gk* hold

have gone over ~ *Gk* finish

have pleasure in ~ *Gk* are being pleased with or agree with

have respect ~ show special honor

having men's persons in admiration ~ admiring men's faces (external status)

havock ~ great destruction

hazarded ~ risked

he ~ male

headlong ~ head first

heady ~ impetuous, rash; willful, headstrong, domineering (*Gk* rash, reckless)

healeth ~ heals ~ 4

heapeth ~ heaps ~ 2

heardest ~ heard ~ 12

hearest ~ hear ~ 11

heareth ~ hears ~ 52

hearken ~ listen carefully

hearkened ~ listened carefully

hearkenedst ~ hearkened ~ 1

hearkeneth ~ hearkens ~ 2

heath ~ small shrub (that grows on the heath or open wasteland)

heaviness ~ grief, sorrow; gloom, dejection; distress, anguish, sorrow

heavy ~ sad, sorrowful; i.e. heavy-hearted; burdened with sorrow

hedge ~ hedge, fence, or barrier

heed ~ careful attention; careful notice; close attention; great care

heifer ~ cow that hasn't given birth

heir ~ inheritor

heirs ~ inheritors

held his peace ~ was silent, kept quiet

held their peace ~ were quiet, kept silent

helm ~ ship's wheel that steers the rudder; tiller

helpeth ~ helps ~ 4

helve ~ handle of a tool, esp of an ax or hatchet

hemlock ~ poisonous plant; poison from that plant

hence ~ from this time or place; from here; away; here

henceforth ~ from this time forward; from now on; hereafter

henceforward ~ from this time forward; from now on

hereafter ~ after this, in the future, from now on, later

hereby ~ by this (means)

herein ~ in this; in this (matter, place, etc.); in here

hereof ~ of this

heresies ~ teachings or opinions that differ with established religious beliefs (*Gk* bodies of men following their own tenets: sects, parties; dissensions arising from diversity of opinions and aims)

heresy ~ teaching or opinion that differs with established religious belief

heretick ~ heretic: a person who professes a heresy--an opinion or teaching that differs with established church beliefs (*Gk* schismatic, factious person {one who causes splits, divisions, factions, parties in a group because of differing opinions or teachings}; a follower of false doctrine; heretic)

heretofore ~ up until now; until the present; before this

hereunto ~ to this (alt of here to)

herewith ~ by this method or means; hereby

heritage ~ *Obs* inheritance

hew ~ shape by cutting or chopping; cut, chop

hewed ~ shaped by chopping, cutting, carving; chopped, cut

hewers ~ choppers, cutters

heweth ~ hews: cuts, chops

hewn ~ carved, chopped, cut

hid ~ hidden

hidest ~ hide ~ 5 ~ hides ~ 1

hideth ~ hides ~ 16

highminded ~ *Arc* haughty, arrogant, proud

hin ~ ancient Hebrew liquid measure=1.5 gallons

hind ~ female deer in and after its third year, esp a red deer

hinder ~ *Rare* hind, rear; posterior

hindereth ~ hinders ~ 1

hindermost ~ *Arc* farthest to the rear, last

hindmost ~ farthest back, farthest to the rear, last

hinds ~ female deer in & after the third year, esp red deer

hire ~ wages, payment

hireling ~ someone for hire; mercenary; hired man

hires ~ payment, wages

hirest ~ hire ~ 1

his own self ~ himself

his state ~ i.e. its proper condition

hither ~ here; to or toward this place

hitherto ~ unto this time or place; up to this point; to now; previously

hoar ~ gray or white with age; white, gray, grayish-white (short for hoary)

hoised ~ *Obs* variant of hoisted

hold ~ *Obs* stronghold (*Heb* cellar; *Gk* prison)

hold ~ take, i.e. consider

hold his peace ~ be quiet, keep silent

hold not thy peace ~ be not silent

hold their peace ~ remain silent, be quiet

hold thy peace ~ be quiet

holden ~ held or held by (*Arc* pp of hold): i.e. covered

holdest me for ~ i.e. treat me as

holdest ~ hold ~ 6

holdeth ~ holds ~ 9

holpen ~ helped (*Arc* or *Dial* pp of help)

honest ~ honorable, respectable; commendable

honestly ~ *Gk* decently

honesty ~ *Obs* respectability; purity

honour ~ honor ~ 146

honourable ~ honorable ~ 30

honoured ~ honored ~ 9

honourest ~ honour, ~ honor ~ 1

honoureth ~ honours,, ~ honors ~ 9

honours ~ honors ~ 1

hopeth ~ hopes ~ 1

horn ~ emblem of glory, strength, and honor

horseleach ~ aquatic blood-sucking worm differing from the common leach in its larger size and in the formation of its jaws

hosen ~ hose, stockings (*Arc* plural of hose) {*Heb* garment, tunic, coat?: meaning is dubious}

host ~ army, hostile force

hough ~ disable{d} by cutting the sinew or tendon of the hock-- the joint in an animal's hind leg corresponding to the human ankle; hamstring (hough{ed}= *Arc* sp of hock{ed})

houghed ~ disabled by cutting the sinew or tendon of the hock-- the joint in an animal's hind leg corresponding to the human ankle; hamstrung (houghed=*Arc* sp of hocked)

householder ~

householder ~ person who owns or maintains a house alone or as head of the household or family; i.e. lord of the manor; owner or master of a house

how hardly ~ *Rare* with how much difficulty or effort

how many soever ~ however many

howbeit ~ *Arc* nevertheless, be that as it may; however

howsoever ~ however (emphatic)

humbledst ~ humbled ~ 1

humbleth ~ humbles ~ 7

hungerbitten ~ bitten or pinched with hunger; starved, famished

hungered ~ was hungry

huntest ~ hunt ~ 2

hunteth ~ hunts ~ 1

hurleth ~ hurls ~ 1

hurt ~ harm; injury (of tempest-caused violence)

husbandman ~ *Arc* farmer

husbandmen ~ *Arc* farmers

husbandry ~ farming; *Gk* cultivated field, tillage

hypocrisy ~ pretending to be what one is not

hypocrite ~ one who pretends to be better than he is

hypocrites ~ ones pretending to be better than they are; pretenders

idle ~ worthless, useless; *Gk* lazy

idols ~ false gods

ignominy ~ dishonor, disgrace, shame

ill savour ~ bad savor: bad taste or smell

ill ~ evil, bad; badly, poorly

ill favoured ~ bad looking

illuminated ~ enlightened

imagery ~ images collectively (*Heb* carved figures, idols)

imaginations ~ foolish notions; evil plans

imagineth ~ imagines ~ 1
immutability ~ unchangeableness
immutable ~ unchangeable; never changing or varying; unalterable; fixed
impart ~ give
impediment ~ defect, obstruction
impenitent ~ unrepentant
imperious ~ domineering, overbearing, dominant; arrogant
implacable ~ unappeasable, irreconcilable; relentless
implead ~ sue in a court of justice, arraign; accuse; bring charges against
importunity ~ troublesome persistence in insisting or demanding
impotent ~ not powerful, helpless, weak
impudent ~ shamelessly bold or disrespectful, insolent; *Obs* immodest, shameless
impute ~ credit(s)
imputed ~ credited
imputed ~ credited, counted
imputeth ~ imputes: ascribes, credits
imputing ~ crediting, counting
in time past ~ *Gk* once, formerly
in ~ i.e. in the
in ~ i.e. treat . . . As an
in respect of ~ *Obs* in comparison with
in the ear ~ i.e. ripening, forming ears
inasmuch as ~ seeing that, since, because; to the extent that
incensed ~ angry
incline ~ bow or bend down
inclined ~ bent over, stooped down
inclineth ~ inclines ~ 1

incontinency ~ inability to contain or restrain oneself; lack of self-control
incontinent ~ unable to contain or restrain oneself; unrestrained; uncontrolled
increasest ~ increase ~ 1
increaseth ~ increases ~ 15
indeed ~ truly, really, in reality
indignation ~ wrath, anger
inditing ~ *Obs* uttering, suggesting, or inspiring a form of words which is to be repeated or written down; dictating; *Arc* expressing or describing in prose or verse; putting in writing, composing, writing
infallible ~ dependable, reliable, certain
infamy ~ shame, disgrace, reproach, very bad reputation
infidel ~ non-believer; one who is unfaithful or unbelieving toward faith or duty
infirmities ~ weaknesses
infirmity ~ *Gk* weakness
infolding ~ enfolding (variant): wrapping up in folds, enveloping, enclosing
inhabitest ~ inhabit ~ 1
inhabiteth ~ inhabits ~ 2
inheriteth ~ inherits ~ 1
iniquity ~ lawlessness
iniquity ~ injustice
injurious ~ likely to cause injury; harmful; offensive or abusive; slanderous or libelous (*Gk* insolent; one who, uplifted with pride, either heaps insulting language upon others or does them some shameful act of wrong)

inkhorn ~ small container made of horn or other material formerly used to hold ink; inkwell

innumerable multitude ~ uncountable crowd

innumerable ~ uncountable

inordinate affection ~ uncontrolled passions

inordinate ~ excessive, unrestrained

inquisition ~ investigation, examination, inquiry

insomuch ~ to such a degree or extent; in as much; so; with that

instant ~ urgent, insistent, persistent; earnest

instantly ~ *Arc* urgently, insistently, persistently; earnestly

insurrection ~ rebellion, revolt

intelligence ~ knowledge, understanding, insight; information

intendest ~ intend ~ 1

intent ~ purpose, intention

intents ~ intentions, purposes

intermeddle ~ *Obs* concern himself with (*Heb* share, have fellowship with)

intermeddleth ~ *Arc* of intermeddles: gets mixed-up with; *Obs* concerns himself with

intreat ~ *Arc* variant of entreat: beg, beseech, implore

intreated ~ *Arc* sp entreated: earnestly asked, begged, implored; i.e. heard and answered; plead with

intruding ~ entering (without permission)

inventions ~ plans, schemes, designs, devices, contrivances

inward ~ *Obs* intimate, close, confidential: belonging to the inner circle of one's acquaintances or friends

inwards ~ entrails, guts, inner or interior organs

isle ~ island, esp a small one; *Heb* coast, shore, region, island

isles ~ coasts, shores, regions, islands

issue ~ flow out, discharge; spring out

issue ~ outflow: offspring, children

issued ~ flowed

issues ~ outflowings

jacinth ~ reddish-orange gemstone

jasper ~ variously colored precious stone: either purple, blue, green, or brass; clear jasper

jeoparded ~ endangered, risked (*rare* form of jeopardized)

jeopardy ~ risk of loss, harm, peril, death, or injury; great danger

Jesus ~ i.e. Joshua (*Heb* equivalent of Jesus)

Jewry ~ *Obs* name for Judea

joinings ~ *Heb* clamps, fittings, bindings, joints

Jonas ~ Jonah ~ 12

jot ~ smallest letter of the Hebrew alphabet; little bit of something

joyed we ~ we rejoiced

jubile ~ time of rejoicing or celebration

judgest ~ judge ~ 8

judgeth ~ judges: examines, discerns

judgment ~ justice

just ~ righteous; i.e. to be just

justified ~ *Gk* shown or declared righteous (by); *Obs* acknowledged as true or genuine

justifieth ~ justifies ~ 4

justify ~ declare(s) righteous
justle ~ variant of jostle: bump, or push (as in a crowd)
keep under ~ *Gk* beat black & blue; discipline by hardships
keep ~ guard(s), protect(s)
keeper of the prison ~ *Gk* jailer or keeper of a prison
keeper ~ guardian, protector; caretaker; watchman, gamekeeper
keepers ~ guards
keepest ~ keep ~ 4
keepeth ~ guards, protects
keepeth ~ keeps: guards
kept holyday ~ held a religious festival or feast
kept ~ guarded, protected; celebrated; i.e. stayed in
kerchiefs ~ cloths used to cover women's heads (*Heb* veils)
kernels ~ seeds contained within any fruit
kid ~ baby or young goat (prepared for a meal)
kids ~ young or baby goats
kill ~ *Heb* murder
killedst ~ killed ~ 2
killest ~ kill ~ 2
killeth ~ kills ~ 23
kin ~ kinfolk, relatives, family
kindle ~ stir up; ignite; catch fire
kindleth ~ kindles ~ 3
kindred ~ family
kindreds ~ families, tribes
kine ~ cows, cattle
kinsfolk ~ *Obs* kinfolk: family, relatives
kinsfolks ~ kinfolk: relatives
kinsman ~ relative (male)
kinsmen ~ relatives (male)
kinswoman ~ female relative

knew ~ recognized
knew ~ knew (sexually)
knewest ~ knew ~ 10
knit ~ tied; bound, knotted
knocketh ~ knocks ~ 4
knop ~ knob; esp a knob-like ornament
knops ~ knobs; esp knob-like ornaments: knobs= rounded lumps or protuberances
know the uttermost ~ *Gk* know accurately or ascertain exactly
know ~ know (sexually)
knowest ~ know ~ 89
knoweth ~ knows ~ 104
known ~ known (sexually)
labour ~ labor ~ 88
laboured ~ labored ~ 19
labourer ~ laborer ~ 2
labourers ~ laborers ~ 9
laboureth ~ labours, ~ labors ~ 5
labouring ~ laboring ~ 4
labours ~ labors ~ 13
lack of service ~ *Gk* deficiency or poverty of charitable giving
lackest ~ lack ~ 2
lacketh ~ lacks ~ 5
lade ~ load, burden down
laded ~ loaded, burdened down
laden ~ loaded, burdened down (Rare)
ladeth ~ lades: loads, burdens down (Rare)
lading ~ loading, burdening; load, burden (Rare)
laid to their charge ~ credited to them
laid ~ added: joined, gathered; taken
laid ~ placed in a resting position
laidst ~ laid ~ 1
lament ~ mourn, grieve; feel deep sorrow or express it by weeping or wailing

lamentation ~ wailing, weeping, mourning

lance ~ spear, javelin

lancets ~ small spears, javelins; darts

languish ~ pine away, grown weak

languished ~ became weak; drooped

languisheth ~ languishes: loses vigor or vitality; droops; wastes away

languishing ~ sickness, weakness

lanterns ~ encased torches

lappeth ~ laps ~ 2

lapwing ~ a bird so named because of its irregular flight and spectacular aerial displays

large ~ i.e. a large sum of

lasciviousness ~ lustfulness, licentiousness, lewdness, wantonness

latchet ~ *Arc* strap/ lace for fastening a sandal/ shoe to foot

lately ~ recently

latter ~ last

laud ~ extol, praise, magnify

laugh them to scorn ~ treat them with extreme, often indignant, contempt or utter disdain

laugh me to scorn ~ treat me with extreme, often indignant, contempt or utter disdain

laughed us to scorn ~ treated us with extreme, often indignant, contempt or utter disdain

laughed to scorn ~ treated with extreme, often indignant, contempt or utter disdain

laughed them to scorn ~ treated them with extreme, often indignant, contempt or utter disdain

laughed him to scorn ~ treated him with extreme, often indignant, contempt or utter disdain

laughed thee to scorn ~ treated thee with extreme, often indignant, contempt or utter disdain

laugheth ~ laughs ~ 1

laver ~ basin, bowl, or other vessel for washing

lavers ~ basins, bowls, or other vessels for washing

lay up ~ treasure up

lay sore ~ *Arc* put great pressure

lay hold on ~ take hold of

layedst ~ layed ~ 1

layest ~ lay ~ 2

layeth ~ lays ~ 18

leadest ~ lead ~ 1

leadeth ~ leads ~ 14

league ~ agreement, alliance(for mutual protection)

leaneth ~ leans ~ 2

leanfleshed ~ lean + fleshed: thin, gaunt, lean

leasing ~ *Obs* lying, falsehood, deceit

least ~ smallest

leave ~ permission

leave caring for ~ stop worrying about

leaven ~ substance used to make bread rise: fermented dough or yeast

leavened ~ with leaven or yeast

leaveneth ~ leavens ~ 2

leaveth ~ leaves ~ 6

leddest ~ led ~ 5

lees ~ dregs, sediment

left off to build ~ i.e. stopped building

left off ~ i.e. stopped

left communing ~ i.e. stopped talking

left ~ stopped, quit

leftest ~ left ~ 1

legion ~ Roman legion: 3,000-6,000 foot soldiers

legions ~ each Roman legion ranged from 3,000-6,000 foot soldiers

lendeth ~ lends ~ 4

lent ~ *Rare* gave, imparted

lentiles ~ lentils ~ 4

let it forth ~ leased, or rented it out

let ~ rented, leased

let ~ rent

let ~ *Arc* hindered

let ~ *Arc* hinder, prevent, obstruct, restrain

letters ~ letters: literature, writings, learning

lettest ~ let ~ 3

letteth ~ lets: *Arc* hinders, prevents, obstructs, restrains

leviathan ~ sea monster (perhaps an extinct dinosaur)

levy a tribute ~ impose a regular obligation of; i.e. collect a tax or collection

levy ~ drafted labor force

lewd ~ *Obs* unprincipled, vicious

lewd ~ showing, or intended to incite, lust or sexual desire, esp in an offensive way; lascivious

lewdness ~ unrestrained lustfulness & eroticism; *Obs* viciousness, villainy

liberal ~ generous, noble

liberality ~ generosity: i.e. gift

liberally ~ generously, freely

libertines ~ freed slaves

licence ~ license: permission, freedom, liberty, opportunity

licketh ~ licks ~ 1

lien ~ *Arc* of lain

liest ~ lie ~ 5

lieth ~ lies/lie ~ 59

lift ~ lifted

liftest ~ lift/lifts ~ 4

lifteth ~ lifts ~ 10

light ~ frivolous, reckless; i.e. small, insignificant

light ~ alight, descend, fall

lighted off ~ *Dial* alighted: got down from or off; dismounted

lighted ~ *Dial* alighted: got down from or off; dismounted; descended and settled; *Rare* came on or upon accidentally

lighten ~ illuminate

lighteneth ~ lightens: shines

lightest ~ light ~ 1

lighteth ~ lights: *Arc* of *Dial* alights: *Rare* comes on or upon accidentally i.e. lands on

lighting down ~ *Dial* alighting: descent

lighting ~ *Dial* alighting: landing

lightly ~ with little motion; gently; *Rare* quickly, speedily; with ease

lightly ~ casually, frivolously, recklessly; with indifference or neglect

lightness ~ recklessness, frivolousness; wantonness

lign aloes ~ lign-aloes: wood of the aloe: yields an aromatic wood called eagle wood; contains an oil used in perfumes, soaps, foods, etc.

ligure ~ precious stone thought to be yellow jacinth

like wise ~ similar manner or way

like unto ~ similar to

like to ~ similar to

like ~ similar; same, exact same; similarly; even, just; i.e. about

like passions ~ similar feelings or emotions

like figure ~ *Gk* anti-type

liken ~ compare

likened ~ compared
liketh ~ likes: *Arc* pleases
likewise ~ in a similar manner
liking ~ *Arc* (in) condition, health
limiteth ~ limits ~ 1
lingered ~ hesitated, continued to stay
lingereth ~ lingers: delays
lintel ~ horizontal support or
    crosspiece over door top
liquor ~ juice, liquid
liquors ~ juices or other liquids (*Heb*
    juices)
listed ~ *Arc* wished, liked, chose
listeth ~ *Arc* wishes, likes, chooses
listeth ~ lists ~ > ~ wills ~ 2
litters ~ enclosed or curtained
    couches mounted on shafts
    and used to carry a single
    passenger; stretchers (*Heb*
    carrying vehicles; liters;
    covered wagons)
little space ~ short time, little while
little of stature ~ small of height: i.e.
    short
little ~ *Gk* for a little (time)
lively ~ vigorous, full of life, living,
    active
livest ~ live ~ 4
liveth ~ lives ~ 96
living ~ life-support: wealth, goods;
    means of sustaining life
living ~ i.e. not stagnant, but fresh
    springing
loadeth ~ loads ~ 1
loathe ~ abhor, detest, feel intense
    dislike, disgust, or hatred for
loatheth ~ loathes: abhors, detests,
    feels intense dislike, disgust,
    or hatred for
loathsome ~ abhorrent, detestable,
    disgusting, nauseating
lodge ~ small (servant) house

lodge ~ rest, live, or stay for a time;
    stay as a guest; pass the night
lodged ~ temporarily housed or
    stayed; rested, stayed for a
    while; temporarily staying
lodgest ~ lodge ~ 1
lodgeth ~ lodges: temporarily stays
lodging ~ place to stay; (temporary)
    living quarters
loft ~ story
loins ~ the hips or lower abdomen
long forbearing ~ i.e. self-restraint
long ~ i.e. for a long
longedst ~ longed ~ 1
longeth ~ longs ~ 4
look ye out ~ find, select
look out ~ i.e. find
lookest ~ look ~ 2
looketh ~ looks ~ 33
looking glass ~ mirror
loose ~ untie, release; *Poetic* break
loosed ~ loosened; released
looseth ~ looses ~ 2
loosing ~ untying, releasing
lop ~ trim
lord ~ master
lordly ~ noble, suitable for a lord;
    regal
loseth ~ loses ~ 1
lot ~ object used to randomly decide;
    i.e. casting lots to randomly
    choose
lot ~ randomly determined task;
    allotment or allotted portion
    (randomly selected)
lothe ~ loathe: feel intense dislike,
    disgust, hatred for; detest, hate
lotheth ~ loathes: despises, hates
lothing ~ loathing: intense disgust
lots ~ objects used to make random
    decisions
lovedst ~ loved ~ 2

lovest ~ love ~ 12
loveth ~ loves ~ 65
loweth ~ lows ~ 1
lowring ~ lowering: dark-clouded;
    overcast, gloomy
lucre ~ illicit, dishonorable, or
    unlawful gain or advantage
lunatick ~ *Arc* for lunatic: moon-
    struck, insane (epileptic ??)
lust ~ strong desire, craving
lust ~ strongly desire or crave
lusted after ~ craved
lusteth ~ lusts: strongly desires
lusts of ~ cravings or strong desires
    for
lusts ~ strong or intense desires,
    cravings
lusty ~ vigorous, lively, robust
mad upon ~ i.e. insane, crazy about
mad ~ insane, crazy; enraged, angry
made ready to our hand ~ *Gk*
    already prepared
made ready ~ prepared
made of none effect ~ *Gk* made vain,
    useless; deprived of force,
    influence, or power;
    inactivated; annulled
made manifest ~ clearly or plainly
    revealed or shown
made insurrection ~ revolted
made haste ~ hurried
made ~ i.e. acted
madest ~ made ~ 10
madness ~ insanity
magnifical ~ *Obs* magnificent:
    renowned, glorious, stately
magnified ~ *Arc* glorified, praised
maid ~ *Poetic* girl or young
    unmarried woman; *Obs* virgin;
    girl or woman servant
maiden ~ *Obs* virgin; young,
    unmarried woman

mail ~ flexible body armor composed
    of small overlapping metal
    rings, loops of chain, or scales
maimed ~ those who are missing an
    important body part like an
    arm, hand, leg, foot, eye, or
    ear
maintainest ~ maintain ~ 1
maintenance ~ sustenance, means of
    support
majesty ~ great splendor
make ready ~ prepare
make merchandise of you ~ *Gk* use
    you for gain
make haste ~ hurry
make fat ~ *Heb* make strong, brace
    up, invigorate
makest ~ make ~ 26
maketh ~ makes ~ 126
malefactor ~ evil doer, criminal
malefactors ~ evil doers, criminals
malice ~ desire to harm others or to
    see others suffer; extreme ill
    will or spite
maliciousness ~ evil
malignity ~ deep-rooted or intense ill-
    will/hatred; great malice
mallows ~ plants that grow in salt
    marshes
mammon ~ Aramaic word for riches:
    riches, money, wealth;
    sometimes personified as a
    false god or an object of
    worship; often regarded as an
    evil influence
man ~ male
man ~ human (*Gk* anthrOpos)
mandrakes ~ poisonous plants of the
    nightshade family formerly
    used in medicine for their
    narcotic and emetic prop-
    erties (*Heb* mandrakes, love-
    apples: thought to excite

sexual desire or encourage procreation)

manifest ~ clearly reveal

manifest ~ plain, clear, obvious,evident; revealed, made known

manifestation ~ revealing: *Gk* unveiling, disclosure

manifested forth ~ clearly or plainly revealed

manifested ~ clearly revealed; made plain; made visible, clear, known

manifestly ~ clearly

manifold temptations ~ various testings

manifold ~ much (of various kinds); many, numerous, abundant; multi-faceted; multi-colored

mankind ~ human males in general; the male sex

manner ~ kind; kinds; kinds of

manners ~ character, behavior

mansions ~ resting, abiding, or dwelling places

manslayers ~ *Gk* man-murderers

mantle ~ loose, sleeveless cloak or cape of varying lengths

mantles ~ loose, sleeveless cloaks or capes of varying lengths

mar ~ disfigure, spoil; damage

Maranatha ~ *Gk* our Lord comes or will come

marchedst ~ marched ~ 1

marishes ~ marshes, swamps, bogs, or other wetlands

mark ~ target

mark ~ note, observe

markest ~ mark ~ 1

marketh ~ marks ~ 3

marred ~ injured or damaged so as to make imperfect, less

attractive: disfigured, spoiled, ruined

marrieth ~ marries ~ 4

mart ~ market place, trading center

marvel ~ wonder

marvelled ~ marveled: wondered

marvellous ~ marvelous: wonderful, amazing

marvellously ~ marvelously

maschil ~ *Heb* poem, song or poem of contemplation

master ~ *Gk* sailing master, helmsman

master ~ teacher, rabbi; owner; lord, head

masteries ~ competition-victories

masters ~ i.e. (authoritative) teachers, esp of Bible

mastery ~ rule, control; victory in competition

matrix ~ womb

matter ~ *Obs* forest, wood, timber

mattock ~ tool used for loosening hard ground or cutting roots; pickax, hoe, plowshare

mattocks ~ tools used for loosening hard ground or cutting roots; pickaxes, hoes, plowshares

maul ~ very heavy hammer, club, or mallet

maw ~ stomach of an animal, esp the fourth stomach of a cud-chewing animal

mayest ~ may ~ 114

me thinketh ~ I think

mean ~ common, obscure, insignificant, low

meanest ~ mean ~ 4

meaneth ~ means ~ 8

measure ~ *Gk* beyond measure: greatly

meat ~ *Arc* food

meats ~ foods

meddleth ~ meddles ~ 1

meet ~ *Rare* proper, fitting, suitable, becoming

meetest ~ fittest, best-qualified

meetest ~ meet ~ 1

meeteth ~ meets ~ 3

melteth ~ melts ~ 7

member ~ body part

members ~ body part(s)

men of low estate ~ *Gk* the ones of lowly condition

men ~ male

merchandise ~ trade: buying & selling; wares

mess ~ portion, share, ration, allotment of food

messes ~ portions, shares, rations, allotments of food

mete ~ *Arc* measure

meted ~ *Arc* measured

meteyard ~ *Arc* measurement (standard of measurement)

midst ~ middle

mightest ~ might ~ 19

milch ~ *Arc* milk-giving

mill ~ place where grain is ground into flour or meal; device that grinds grain

millet ~ a cereal grass whose small grain is used for food in Europe and Asia

millstone ~ either of a pair of large flat stones between which grain or other substances are ground

mincing ~ walking with little steps; affecting daintiness

mind ~ think about, seek

mind ~ way of thinking, mind-set; opinion; i.e. will

minded ~ inclined, disposed, resolved, determined

mindful of ~ remembering

minding ~ intending

mingled ~ mixed, blended, combined

minish ~ *Arc* make or become less; diminish

minished ~ *Arc* made less; diminished

minister unto ~ serve, assist, help with

minister ~ give aid, assistance, help; provide, serve, assist; i.e. promote; *Arc* provide, supply

minister ~ servant, assistant, helper, attendant; *Gk* priest-like servant

minister for ~ serve, assist, help

minister to ~ serve, assist, help

ministered unto him of their substance ~ *Gk* were helping him from their own resources

ministered ~ furnished, supplied

ministered unto ~ served, helped, assisted

ministereth ~ ministers: provides

ministers ~ servants

ministration ~ service, ministry

ministry ~ priestly service

minstrel ~ *Poetic* musician (*Heb* player of a stringed instrument)

minstrels ~ Old *Poetic* musicians (*Gk* flute players)

mire ~ deep mud; wet, soggy ground; bog

mirth ~ joyfulness, merriment, laughter

mischief ~ injury, harm, damage esp done by a person; action or conduct that causes damage or trouble

mischievous ~ harmful, injurious

miserably ~ painfully, wretchedly

mite ~ small brass coin worth about 1/5 of a cent

mites ~ small brass coins each worth about 1/5 of a cent

mitre ~ Brit sp of miter: cap, headband, turban; headdress or other ceremonial headwear

moan ~ lament; mourn over; show grief or pity over

mockest ~ mock ~ 1

mocketh ~ mocks ~ 5

moderation ~ *Gk* gentleness, mildness, fairness

mollified ~ softened, soothed, pacified, made tender

molten ~ formed by melting & casting in mold; metal melted then poured into a mold

more part ~ majority

more a great deal ~ *Gk* much more

more ~ more in number or importance

morrow ~ next day, day following; *Arc* next day, next morning

mortify ~ destroy the vitality or vigor of (*Gk* destroy, kill)

mote ~ speck of dirt or dust; splinter, chip of wood

mount ~ *Obs* raised fortification

mounts ~ *Obs* raised fortifications

mourneth ~ mourns ~ 11

moved with ~ motivated by

moved ~ carried along

moved sedition ~ *Obs* made a revolt or rebellion

movedst ~ moved ~ 1

moveth ~ moves ~ 8

much speaking ~ i.e. many words

much ~ many; very

mufflers ~ kerchiefs, scarves (*Heb* probably veils)

multipliedst ~ multiplied ~ 1

multiplieth ~ multiplies ~ 3

multitude ~ crowd, masses of people; number

multitudes ~ crowds, masses of people

munition ~ *Arc* fortification, stronghold; bulwark, siege-works

munitions ~ *Arc* fortifications, strongholds

murmur ~ grumble, mutter, or mumble complaints

murmured ~ grumbled; complained by muttering; muttered complaints

murmurers ~ grumblers

murmuring ~ grumbling, muttering of complaints; complainings

murmurings ~ muttered or mumbled complaints; grumblings, complainings

murrain ~ any of various infectious cattle-diseases; *Arc* plague, pestilence

muse ~ meditate, think deeply and at length

mused ~ meditated, thought deeply and at length

musick ~ music

musing ~ meditating, thinking deeply and at length

mustered ~ gathered, summoned (for military duty)

mustereth ~ musters: gathers (an army)

nameth ~ names ~ 1

napkin ~ any small cloth or towel; Brit handkerchief (*Gk* handkerchief; a cloth for wiping perspiration from the face and for cleaning the nose and also used in swathing the head of a corpse)

nativity ~ birth, esp of place, time, or conditions
naturally ~ in a natural manner; by nature, innately; *Gk* genuinely, faithfully, sincerely
naught ~ *Obs* worthless, useless (alt sp of nought--nothing)
naughtiness ~ *Obs* wickedness, viciousness, depravity
naughty ~ *Obs* bad, evil
naves ~ wheel-hubs
nay ~ no
necromancer ~ one who claims to foretell the future by alleged communication with the dead; a practicer of black magic, sorcery
needest ~ need ~ 1
needeth ~ needs ~ 6
needlework ~ embroidery, fancywork--ornamental work
needs be ~ of necessity be, necessarily be (i.e. act like)
needs ~ of necessity, necessarily
neesings ~ sneezings, sneezes (*Arc* sp); sneezing
neighbour ~ neighbor ~ 107
neighbours ~ neighbors ~ 21
neighbours' ~ neighbors' ~ 1
neighbour's ~ neighbor's ~ 28
neighed ~ whinnied (made the characteristic horse sound)
neighing ~ whinnying (the characteristic sound of a horse)
neighings ~ whinnyings (the characteristic sounds of a horse)
nephews ~ *Obs* descendants, grandsons (*Heb* progeny, posterity; *Gk* grandchildren, offspring, descendants)
net ~ network or grate

nether ~ lower
nethermost ~ lowest
nigh ~ *Dialect* near; *Dialect* nearly, almost
nigh at hand ~ *Dialect* near+close by; *Gk* near
nigh ~ near100-
nitre ~ Brit sp of niter--sodium nitrate, a cleansing agent (*Heb* natron, nitre, soda, carbonate of soda)
no wise ~ no way
no brawlers ~ free from noisy fights or quarrels
no striker ~ not addicted to striking or hitting
Noe ~ Noah ~ 5
noised abroad ~ rumored, reported far and wide
noised ~ rumored, reported
noisome ~ harmful, injurious to health
none occasion ~ no cause
none ~ no; no one
noontide ~ noon time, noon, midday
notable ~ notorious, infamous; outstanding, remarkable; *Gk* conspicuous
nothing laid to his charge ~ *Gk* not one accusation
notwithstanding ~ greet
nought ~ nothing (var of naught)
nought ~ *Gk* utterly despised, treated with contempt
nourisheth ~ nourishes ~ 1
novice ~ new convert
now of a long time ~ *Gk* from long ago
numberest ~ number ~ 3
nurture ~ the act or process of raising or promoting the development of: training, educating, fostering, etc. (*Gk* the whole

training and education of children {which relates to the cultivation of mind and morals, and employs for this purpose now commands and admonitions, now reproof and punishment; It also includes the training and care of the body.})

obeisance ~ expression of submission, often involving a bow

obeyedst ~ obeyed ~ 2

obeyeth ~ obeys ~ 3

oblation ~ sacrifice or offering

oblations ~ sacrifices or offerings

observation ~ kjv margin: outward show

observest ~ observe ~ 1

observeth ~ observes ~ 1

obtaineth ~ obtains ~ 2

occasion ~ incident; cause; reason; opportunity

occupied ~ traded, bartered, marketed

occupied ~ used

occupiers ~ *Arc* marketers, traders, barterers, exchangers

occupieth ~ occupies: fills

occupy ~ *Arc* market, trade, barter, exchange; i.e. make a profit (with)

occurrent ~ *Arc* occurrence, event, action, incident

odd ~ left over, irregular

odious ~ offensive, disgusting, detestable, repugnant; arousing or deserving hatred or loathing

odour ~ odor ~ 2

odours ~ fragrances

odours ~ odors: *Arc* perfume, incense; sweet smells

of the ranges ~ from the rows, ranks (of soldiers)

of late ~ lately

of above ~ by more than

of his own accord ~ automatically (*Gk* automatos)

of ~ i.e. out of, from; i.e. by; i.e. on; i.e. for a

of ~ for; at; with; by; on; *Gk* according to; *Gk* by

of a child ~ *Gk* from childhood

of a long season ~ for a long time

of a surety ~ i.e. certainly

of a truth ~ truly

offence ~ *Gk* cause of stumbling

offend thee ~ cause (thee) to stumble

offend ~ cause(s) to stumble; *Gk* scandalize(s)

offended ~ caused to stumble; *Gk* scandalized; *Gk* sinned (in)

offereth ~ offers ~ 15

offscouring ~ what is scoured off: filth; refuse cleaned off and thrown away

oft ~ Literary variant of often

oftener ~ more frequently, often

oftentimes ~ *Poetic* of often: often, frequently

ofttimes ~ *Poetic* of often: often, frequently

oil olive ~ i.e. olive oil

oiled ~ moistened with or containing oil

omer ~ Hebrew unit of dry measure c. 1/10 of an ephah

omnipotent ~ all powerful, having unlimited power or authority

on usury ~ at (excessively high) interest

on this wise ~ in this way

on a smoke ~ i.e. covered with smoke

on ~ in

one cubit ~ c. 18 inches

one born out of due time ~ a
    miscarriage
only begotten ~ *Gk* i.e. uniquely-
    related (one): monO-genAs
onycha ~ the operculum (the horny
    plate serving to close the shell
    when the animal is retracted)
    of a marine mollusk which
    emits a penetrating aroma
    when burned
openest ~ open ~ 2
openeth ~ opens ~ 21
opening ~ (of the mind)
operation ~ work, working
operations ~ works, workings
opposest ~ oppose ~ 1
opposeth ~ opposes ~ 1
oppresseth ~ oppresses ~ 5
or ever ~ before
oracle ~ holy of holies in the Jewish
    tabernacle & temple
oracles ~ words or utterances of God
oration ~ formal speech
orator ~ eloquent public speaker
ordaineth ~ ordains ~ 1
order ~ arrangement, instructions
ordereth ~ orders ~ 1
ordinance ~ *Gk* institution; *Arc*
    governmental system
ordinances ~ prescribed practices;
    traditions
Osee ~ Hosea
osprey ~ a large black and white
    diving bird that feeds mainly
    on fish (Heb. Perhaps an
    extinct bird, meaning
    uncertain)
ossifrage ~ Lit. "bone-breaker":
    vulture (*Arc* of Osprey)
ouches ~ brooches or clasps; settings
    for precious stones
ought ~ anything
oughtest ~ ought ~ 4

out of ~ beyond, i.e. before (their)
out ~ spy, catch sight of; see
outgoings ~ extremities, outer limits,
    borders
outlandish ~ *Arc* foreign, alien
outmost ~ outermost, most remote
outwent ~ went before, went ahead,
    preceded
over much ~ too much
over ~ upon
over against ~ on the other side of,
    opposite to; next to, before;
    near; in front of; toward
overcharge ~ overload, overburden
overcharged ~ overloaded,
    overburdened; filled too full
overcometh ~ overcomes ~ 11
overdrive ~ severely drive
overfloweth ~ overflows ~ 1
overlaid ~ lay on top of
overlived ~ outlived, survived (*Obs*)
overmuch ~ too much
overpass ~ pass over
overpast ~ passed over
overplus ~ surplus
overran ~ *Arc* outran
overrunning ~ i.e. overwhelming
overspread ~ scattered, dispersed
overtaketh ~ overtakes ~ 1
overthroweth ~ overthrows ~ 5
overturneth ~ overturns ~ 3
owest ~ owe ~ 4
oweth ~ owes ~ 1
owneth ~ owns ~ 2
pacifieth ~ pacifies ~ 2
paddle ~ small spade or trowel
painful ~ *Arc* laborious, difficult,
    painstaking
paintedst ~ painted ~ 1
pair of balances ~ pair of scales (for
    weighing by balancing)
palestina ~ i.e. Palestine

palmerworm ~ migratory caterpillar

palms ~ palm branches

palsies ~ paralysis of any voluntary muscles as a result of some disorder to nervous system, sometimes accompanied by involuntary tremors

palsy ~ paralysis of any voluntary muscles as a result of some disorder to the nervous system, sometimes accompanied with involuntary tremors

pangs ~ sudden, sharp, and brief pains--physical or emo-tional; spasms of distress

panteth ~ pants ~ 3

paps ~ *Arc* nipples or teats (*Heb* breasts; *Gk* breasts)

paramours ~ lovers, esp the illicit sexual partners of a married man or woman

parched ~ dried up with heat; hot and dry; dried, roasted

parchments ~ i.e. scrolls made of animal skins

pardoneth ~ pardons ~ 1

parlour ~ reception room, formal sitting room: alt spell parlor

parlour ~ parlor ~ 5

parlours ~ reception rooms, formal sitting rooms: alt spell parlors)

parlours ~ parlors ~ 1

part ~ side or party (in a conflict)

part ~ divide

partakest ~ partake ~ 1

parted ~ divided into parts; separated, divided

parteth ~ parts ~ 3

particularly ~ specifically

partition ~ separation, division

passages ~ fords

passedst ~ passed ~ 1

passest ~ pass ~ 5

passeth ~ passes: surpasses; *Gk* surpasses

passion ~ suffering or agony

passover ~ *Gk* Passover lamb

past feeling ~ *Gk* callous; insensible to pain

pastors ~ shepherds

pate ~ head, esp the top or crown of the head

patriarch ~ father & ruler of a family or tribe

patrimony ~ inheritance from one's father or ancestors

pavilion ~ large tent, usually with a peaked top

pavilions ~ large tents with a peaked top

paweth ~ paws ~ 1

payed ~ paid ~ 2

payeth ~ pays ~ 1

peculiar ~ special, particular; belonging exclusively

pence ~ *Gk* denarius--Roman silver coin: each equal to c. a day's labor

penny ~ *Gk* denarius--a Roman silver coin: equal to c. a day's labor

pennyworth ~ *Gk* denarius--Roman silver coins: each equal to c. a day's labor

pentecost ~ the second of the three great Jewish feasts, cele-brated at Jerusalem yearly, the seventh week after the Passover, in grateful recognition of the completed harvest; fiftieth day after Passover

penury ~ lack of money, property, or necessities; extreme poverty; destitution

peradventure ~ *Arc* perhaps, possibly; by chance
perceivest ~ perceive ~ 2
perceiveth ~ perceives ~ 3
perdition ~ damnation, utter ruin, destruction
performeth ~ performs ~ 4
peril ~ danger
perilous ~ dangerous
perils ~ dangers
perish ~ be destroyed
perisheth ~ perishes ~ 9
perjured persons ~ ones who lie under oath
pernicious ~ destructive, hurtful, *Rare* wicked
perpetual ~ perpetually: permanently, without interruption
perplexed ~ puzzled, confused, doubtful
perplexity ~ uncertainty, confusion, bewilderment
persecutest ~ persecute ~ 6
perseverance ~ continued, patient effort; persistence
persuadest ~ persuade ~ 1
persuadeth ~ persuades ~ 2
pertaineth ~ pertains ~ 7
perverse ~ wicked; stubbornly contrary, obstinate; corrupt(ed); deviated from what is right; twisted away from the good
perverseness ~ persistence in error or fault; stubbornness; deviation from what is right and good
pervert ~ twist, distort; corrupt
perverteth ~ perverts ~ 5
pestilence ~ infectious, deadly disease; plague
pestilences ~ deadly contagious diseases
pestilent ~ dangerous, troublesome

petition ~ solemn request to superior
phylacteries ~ boxes for Scripture
pictures ~ images carved in relief
pierceth ~ pierces ~ 1
piety ~ affectionate loyalty & respect
pilled ~ peeled (British Dialect)
pine ~ waste
pineth ~ pines: wastes
pinnacle ~ high point, peak
pipe ~ flute, pan-pipe
piped unto ~ played the flute for
piped ~ played the flute or pan-pipe
pipers ~ flute players
pipes ~ flutes
piss ~ urine (formerly acceptable, now Vulgar)
pisseth ~ urinates (once acceptable; now Vulgar)
pitch ~ black, sticky waterproofing material; water-proofing sealer
pitch ~ smear or cover with pitch, tar
pitieth ~ pities ~ 3
pitiful ~ *Arc* full of pity or compassion; merciful
place ~ space, room; [your] place; i.e. ground
plague ~ affliction, calamity
plagues ~ afflictions or calamities
plaiting ~ braiding, folding, weaving (pleating)
plantedst ~ planted ~ 2
planteth ~ plants ~ 5
plat ~ small plot or portion of land
platted ~ braided, weaved, or woven
play ~ sport; *Obs* engage in sexual activity
playedst ~ played ~ 2
playeth ~ plays ~ 1
pleadeth ~ pleads ~ 3
pleaseth ~ pleases ~ 6

pledge ~ object given to secure a debt; security, down-payment; collateral

pledges ~ objects that guarantee a promise

plenteous ~ plentiful

plotteth ~ plots ~ 1

ploweth ~ plows ~ 1

plowshares ~ cutting blade of moldboard plows

pluck ~ snatch, take by violence

plucked asunder ~ pulled apart or into pieces or parts

plucketh ~ plucks ~ 1

pluckt ~ plucked ~ 1

plummet ~ plumb bob'

poll ~ trim, clip, cut-off (the hair of)

polled ~ (*Arc*) shaved, cut the hair (on the head)

polls ~ heads; head counts--census

polluted ~ profaned, defiled, desecrated

pommels ~ rounded kn*obs* (*Heb* bowl-shaped portions of the capitals of temple pillars)

pomp ~ stately or showy display

pondered ~ thought deeply about

pondereth ~ ponders ~ 3

porter ~ door or gate keeper

porters ~ door or gate keepers

possessest ~ possess ~ 1

possesseth ~ possesses ~ 2

possessions ~ fields

post ~ runner, courier

posts ~ runners, couriers

potentate ~ someone having great power: sovereign, ruler, king, dictator

potsherd ~ fragment or broken piece of pottery

pottage ~ contents of a pot: stew, soup, porridge

pound ~ originally a pound weight of silver: OT 1 pound=300 shekels; NT 100 pounds=1 talent, 1 pound=10.33 oz or 300 g

pouredst ~ poured ~ 1

poureth ~ pours ~ 11

pourtray ~ portray: display

pourtrayed ~ portrayed: pictured

power ~ ability; *Gk* authority: symbol or sign of authority

powers ~ authorities

praiseth ~ praises ~ 1

prating ~ foolish, idle, boastful, excessive, or vain talking

pray ~ *Rare* earnestly ask or beg, implore, beseech

prayed ~ asked, begged

prayest ~ pray ~ 2

prayeth ~ prays ~ 7

praying ~ begging

preachest ~ preach ~ 1

preacheth ~ preaches ~ 3

predestinate ~ predetermine,

predestinated ~ decreed beforehand; foreordained

preparedst ~ prepared ~ 1

preparest ~ prepare ~ 3

prepareth ~ prepares ~ 3

presbytery ~ assembly of elders

preservest ~ preserve ~ 2

preserveth ~ preserves ~ 8

press ~ *Arc* crowd, throng

pressed upon ~ i.e. plead with, strongly urged

presseth ~ presses ~ 2

pressfat ~ wine-press, wine vat

presumptuous sins ~ sins of arrogance or overconfidence

presumptuous ~ arrogant, overconfident

presumptuously ~ boldly, arrogantly; overconfidently; insolently, defiantly

pretence ~ false show or claim; pretext

prevailed ~ i.e. overwhelmed

prevailest ~ prevail ~ 1

prevaileth ~ prevails

prevent ~ *Obs* come or go before; precede, anticipate

prevented ~ *Obs* come or gone before; preceded, anticipated

preventest ~ prevent: *Obs* come or go before; precede, anticipate

prey ~ plunder; hunt or kill another animal; victimize

prey ~ plunder; animal hunted or killed by another animal; victim; *Heb* plunder; gift, prize

pricks ~ *Arc* any of various pointed objects as thorns, goads, etc

principal ~ most important; chief, main; head

principalities ~ princely ranks, dignities, or jurisdictions; princely territories or countries

principality ~ princely rank, dignity, or jurisdiction; princely territory or country

principles ~ basics, fundamentals

printed ~ inscribed

prised ~ prized (Brit): priced, valued, appraised

prisoner ~ *Gk* bound, in chains

privily ~ *Arc* privately, secretly

privy to ~ *Arc* privately informed about

privy ~ *Arc* private

proceedeth ~ proceeds ~ 11

proclaimeth ~ proclaims ~ 1

procureth ~ procures: gets (by effort); obtains

profane ~ make common or unholy: debase, desecrate, defile

profane ~ common, unholy; defiled, debased

profaned ~ made common or unholy: debased, desecrated, defiled

profaneth ~ makes common: debases, desecrates, defiles

profaning ~ making common or unholy: debasing, defiling, desecrating

profited ~ i.e. increased, advanced

profiteth ~ profits ~ 6

progenitors ~ ancestors, forefathers

prognosticators ~ predictors, forecasters, foretellers

prolongeth ~ prolongs ~ 2

promisedst ~ promised ~ 3

proof ~ *Obs* tested or proved strength

proof ~ trial, testing, & approval

proper tongue ~ own language

proper good ~ *Heb* property

proper ~ own; *Arc* fine-looking, handsome

prophesieth ~ prophesies ~ 7

propitiation ~ satisfaction, appeasement, expiation

proselyte ~ convert to Judaism

proselytes ~ converts to Judaism

prospereth ~ prospers ~ 4

prosperously ~ successfully

prosperously effected ~ *Heb* caused to prosper

prostitute ~ sell the services of; *Heb* defile, pollute

protest ~ solemnly affirm, declare

prove ~ test, try; try and approve; approve (after trial); verify, substantiate; give evidence; give evidence for; show

proved ~ tested, tried; tried, and approved; shown, demonstrated

provender ~ fodder, feed; dry animal food

proveth ~ proves ~ 1

providence ~ provision, foresight

provideth ~ provides ~ 2

proving ~ approving

provocation ~ defiance

provoke ~ incite, stir-up

provokedst ~ provoked ~ 1

provoketh ~ provokes ~ 3

prudence ~ practical understanding

psalteries ~ ancient stringed instruments

psaltery ~ ancient stringed instrument

publican ~ tax collector for the Roman Empire

publicans ~ tax collectors for the Roman Empire

publick ~ public ~ 1

publickly ~ publicly ~ 2

publish ~ proclaim, announce

published ~ proclaimed, announced

publisheth ~ publishes ~ 4

puffeth ~ puffs: sniffs, pants, blows

pulpit ~ raised platform

pulse ~ edible seeds of peas, beans, lentils, and similar plants having pods

purchase to ~ i.e. obtain for

purely ~ thoroughly, completely

purged ~ cleansed, purified

purgeth it ~ rids it of impurities, foreign matter, or undesirable elements

purgeth ~ purges ~ 1

purifieth ~ purifies ~ 2

purloining ~ stealing

purple ~ purple (robe)

purposed ~ decided, intended; planned

purposeth ~ purposes ~ 1

purse ~ money bag or money pouch; *Gk* money-belt

purses ~ small bags or pouches for carrying money; *Gk* hollow belts for money-hiding

pursueth ~ pursues ~ 8

purtenance ~ *Arc* the viscera (internal organs) of an animal

put off ~ *Gk* untie

put in trust ~ entrusted

put to ~ put forth, use, exert

put you in remembrance ~ remind you

put her away ~ i.e. divorce her

put away ~ i.e. divorced

putrifying ~ becoming putrid (foul-smelling): rotting, decaying, decomposing (*Heb* fresh, new)

puttest ~ put ~ 7

putteth ~ puts ~ 30

putting you in remembrance ~ *Gk* remind(ing) you

putting you in mind ~ reminding you

pygarg ~ an antelope (or gazelle) with a white rump

quarrel ~ cause for dispute or conflict; angry, resentful grudge or disagreement

quarries ~ kjv margin=graven images

quarter ~ region, district, place

quarters ~ regions, districts, places

quaternions ~ set of four: *Gk* a guard consisting of four soldiers (for among the Romans this was the usual number of the guard to which the custody of captives and prisoners was entrusted; two soldiers were confined with the prisoner and two kept guard outside). Four quaternions of soldiers would be used to guard one all night, one for each of the four night watches.

quench ~ extinguish, put out

quenched ~ extinguished, put out

question ye ~ *Gk* are ye discussing or disputing

quick ~ rapid; *Arc* living, alive

quicken ~ revive, enliven, animate; make alive

quickened ~ revived, enlivened; made alive

quickeneth ~ quickens: revives, enlivens; makes alive

quickening ~ life-giving; reviving, enlivening

quieteth ~ quiets ~ 1

quit you ~ *Arc* conduct yourselves: i.e. act

quit ~ free (from obligation); *Arc* conduct (oneself)

quite ~ completely, totally

raca ~ empty-head, senseless

rageth ~ rages ~ 1

rail ~ speak bitterly or reproachfully (against, at, or on)

railed on ~ spoke bitterly or reproachfully against

railed ~ spoke bitterly or reproachfully (against)

railer ~ one characterized by bitter, reproachful, abusive speech: reviler

railing ~ bitter, reproachful, abusive speech

railings ~ bitter, reproachful, abusive speeches

raiment ~ *Arc* clothing, attire, apparel, dress: i.e. covering

raiseth ~ raises ~ 8

raising up ~ stirring up, inciting

rampart ~ bank of earth raised around a fort as a bulwark or defense

ranges ~ i.e. cooking furnaces, stoves

ranges ~ rows, ranks (of soldiers)

ranging ~ roaming, wandering

rank ~ full-grown, robust, ripe, healthy

rase ~ raze: demolish (Brit sp)

rash ~ reckless, too hasty

rattleth ~ rattles ~ 1

ravening ~ greedily searching for prey; plundering, tearing

ravenous ~ greedily or wildly hungry; voracious or famished

ravin ~ greedily devour (alt sp of raven)

ravin ~ torn remnants (alt sp of raven)

ravished ~ seized, carried away by force; raped; enraptured; transported with joy, delight

reacheth ~ reaches ~ 14

readest ~ read ~ 2

readeth ~ reads ~ 4

ready ~ willing

reapest ~ reap ~ 2

reapeth ~ reaps ~ 4

rear up ~ raise, build, erect

rear ~ raise, build, erect

reared ~ raised, i.e. set

reason ~ i.e. reasonable; *Gk* pleasing, agreeable

reason ye ~ *Gk* are ye reasoning

rebellest ~ rebel ~ 2

rebuketh ~ rebukes ~ 4

receipt of custom ~ place where tribute, tax, or toll was collected

receivedst ~ received ~ 1

receiveth ~ receives ~ 37

reckon ~ consider, count

reckoned ~ counted, calculated, credited

reckoneth ~ reckons: settles accounts

reckoning ~ accounting

recompence ~ repayment, reward, compensation

recompences ~ repayments, rewards, compensations

recompense ~ repay, reward, compensate

recompensed ~ repaid, rewarded, compensated

recompensest ~ recompense: repay, reward, compensate

recompensing ~ repaying, rewarding, compensating

record ~ witness

recount ~ call to mind, recall; count again

redeemed ~ bought back

redeemedst ~ redeemed ~ 1

redeemeth ~ redeems ~ 2

redound ~ *Arc* overflow; surge up

reformation ~ re-forming; restoring; making straight

refrain ~ *Arc* restrain, curb

refrained ~ restrained

refraineth ~ refrains ~ 1

refresheth ~ refreshes ~ 1

refuge ~ place of safety or protection; shelter from danger

refuse ~ worthless, useless, rejected

refusedst ~ refused ~ 1

refuseth ~ refuses ~ 9

regard **not** ~ do not turn aside to

regard ~ consider, hold in affection or respect; *Arc* show concern for

regarded **them** **not** ~ ignored them

regarded ~ valued; cared for; looked upon

regardest ~ regard ~ 4

regardeth ~ regards: considers; is concerned for; attentively observes; *Arc* shows concern for

regarding ~ considering

regeneration ~ new birth

rehearse ~ recite, repeat, relate, narrate

rehearsed ~ recited, repeated, related, narrated

reignest ~ reign ~ 1

reigneth ~ reigns ~ 13

reins ~ *Arc* kidneys or kidney region; loins: considered as the source of emotions, feelings, or affections

rejecteth ~ rejects ~ 1

rejoicest ~ rejoice ~ 1

rejoiceth ~ rejoices ~ 18

release to ~ holiday for

relieveth ~ relieves ~ 1

remainest ~ remain ~ 2

remaineth ~ remains ~ 37

rememberest ~ remember ~ 2

remembereth ~ remembers ~ 5

remembrance ~ memory

remission ~ forgiveness, pardon

remit ~ forgive, pardon

remitted ~ forgiven, pardoned

remnant ~ remainder, rest

removeth ~ removes ~ 5

rend ~ tear, pull apart, split, or rip up with violence

render ~ repay, return, give, present; pay off, repay; give back, return

rendered ~ paid back, repaid; gave back

renderest ~ render: pay back, repay, give

rendereth ~ renders: gives

rending ~ tearing, ripping

renewest ~ renew ~ 2

renown ~ great fame or reputation; celebrity

rent ~ tore (tore, torn, tare), pulled apart, split, or ripped up violence

rentest ~ rent: tear, rip

repayeth ~ repays ~ 1

repeateth ~ repeats ~ 1

repent ~ change your mind (about sin, self, & the Savior)

repentance ~ a change of mind (toward sin, self, & the Savior)

repented them ~ i.e. sorrowed

repented ~ grieved, sorrowed; dissatisfied

repentest ~ repent ~ 1

repenteth ~ repents: sorrows, grieves, saddens; dissatisfies

replenish ~ *Arc* fill; populate; fill or supply with people

repliest ~ reply ~ 1

reproach ~ shame, scorn, disgrace; *Obs* object of blame or scorn

reproached ~ scorned, reviled

reproachest ~ reproach ~ 1

reproacheth ~ reproaches: finds fault with, rebukes

reprobate ~ rejected, condemned, unapproved (after failing a test)

reprobates ~ ones rejected, condemned, unapproved (after failing the test)

reprove ~ rebuke, censure; *Obs* refute, disprove; *Obs* convince, convict

reproved ~ disapproved, censured

reproveth ~ reproves ~ 4

reputation ~ *Gk* honor

reputed ~ considered

requirest ~ require ~ 1

requireth ~ requires ~ 2

requite ~ pay back, reward; avenge, retaliate

requited ~ paid back, repaid; rewarded; avenged, retaliated

requiting ~ paying back, rewarding; avenging

rereward ~ *Arc* rearward: rear-guard- -military detachment that protects the rear of a main body or force

rescueth ~ rescues ~ 1

resemble ~ compare

reserveth ~ reserves ~ 2

residue of ~ rest of [the]

residue ~ rest, remainder

resisteth ~ resists ~ 4

resort ~ go (for help, comfort, aid, or support); *Gk* assemble, come together

resorted ~ came, went (for help, aid, comfort); customarily or often went; went (on a regular basis)

respect of persons ~ improper favor, partiality, or favoritism

respecteth ~ respects ~ 2

respite ~ delay, postponement; relief

restest ~ rest ~ 1

resteth ~ rests ~ 4

restitution ~ reimbursement, restoration

restoreth ~ restores ~ 2

restrainest ~ restrain ~ 1

retained ~ kept

retaineth ~ retains ~ 3

retire ~ retreat

retired ~ retreated

returneth ~ returns ~ 7

revealeth ~ reveals ~ 6

revelation ~ unveiling

revellings ~ noisy feasts; loud merry- making; or any kind of disorderly or immoral festival

revenger ~ punisher

revengeth ~ revenges ~ 2
reverence ~ respect, honor
revile ~ curse, verbally abuse
reviled ~ used abusive language at (or against); abused with contemptuous words; verbally abused
revilest thou ~ Are you verbally abusing
revilest ~ revile ~ 1
revilings ~ verbal abuse, name calling
rewardeth ~ rewards ~ 6
ribband ~ cord, twisted-thread; *Arc* form of ribbon)
rid ~ *Arc* deliver, rescue; free; remove
riddance ~ removal, clearance; deliverance
rideth ~ rides ~ 7
rie ~ rye (*Heb* spelt--a wheat-like crop planted and harvested in fall or spring)
rifled ~ plundered, pillaged, ransacked
right ~ very, extremely
rightly dividing ~ *Gk* right-cutting: properly handling
rigour ~ rigor: harshness, severity, difficulty
ringstraked ~ *Obs* ring-streaked: having bands of color around the body
riot ~ *Rare* participate in: wild, loose living; debauchery; unrestrained revelry
riot ~ *Rare* wild, loose living; debauchery; unrestrained revelry; wild, noisy feast or revel
rioting ~ *Rare* loose living, debauchery; unrestrained revelry
riotous ~ shamelessly immoral, debauched; profligate;

extremely wasteful; unrestrained
risest ~ rise ~ 2
riseth ~ rises ~ 14
rising ~ i.e. swelling, abscess, tumor, boil
road ~ *Obs* raid, invasion (*Heb* a dash)
roareth ~ roars ~ 3
roast ~ roasted
roasteth ~ roasts ~ 2
robbeth ~ robs ~ 1
roe ~ small, agile, graceful Asiatic and European deer
roes ~ small, agile, graceful Asiatic and European deer
roll of a book ~ i.e. scroll
roll ~ i.e. scroll
rolleth ~ rolls ~ 1
room ~ place (at the table); place, position; *Obs* place
rooms ~ places
round about ~
round about ~ all around; i.e. on either side of
rouse ~ wake
rovers ~ wanderers, i.e. nomads
ruddy ~ reddish, in a healthy way; healthy, reddish color
rude ~ unlearned, ignorant: unskilled in any art
rudiments ~ elements, fundamental principles
rue ~ shrubby plant with bitter tasting leaves formerly used in medicine
rulest ~ rule ~ 2
ruleth ~ rules ~ 14
ruling ~ managing
rumour ~ rumor ~ ~ 10
rumours ~ rumors ~ 2
runnest ~ run ~ 1
runneth ~ runs ~ 11

rush ~ grass-like aquatic plant with hollow stems found on banks of rivers, ponds, and marshes

rushes ~ grass-like aquatic plants with hollow stems found on banks of rivers, ponds, and marshes

rusheth ~ rushes ~ 1

sackbut ~ medieval wind instrument, forerunner of the trom-bone (*Heb* a triangular musical instrument with four strings, similar to a lyre)

sacrificedst ~ sacrificed ~ 1

sacrificeth ~ sacrifices ~ 6

said ~ before mentioned

saint ~ holy one

saints ~ holy ones

saith ~ says ~ 1262

saltness ~ saltiness

salutation ~ greeting

salutations ~ greetings

salute ~ greet or welcome with friendly words or respectful gestures

saluted ~ greeted

saluteth ~ greets

saluteth ~ salutes ~ 5

sanctification ~ setting apart, consecration; holiness, purification

sanctified ~ set apart, made holy; consecrated; purified, separated

sanctifieth ~ makes holy, sets apart

sanctifieth ~ sanctifies ~ 4

sanctify ~ set apart, make holy; consecrate; purify, cleanse

sardine ~ red stone from Sardius: (*Gk* a precious stone: either a carnelian [flesh colored] or a sard [red])

satest ~ sat ~ 2

satiate ~ *Rare* satisfied to the full; gratified completely

satiate ~ *Rare* satisfy to the full; gratify completely

satiated ~ *Rare* satisfied to the full; gratified completely

satisfaction ~ reparation, ransom, bribe

satisfiest ~ satisfy ~ 1

satisfieth ~ satisfies ~ 3

satyr ~ in mythology: a minor woodland deity (companion of Bacchus) depicted as having the pointed ears, legs, and short horns of a goat, the head and body of a man, and a fondness for unrestrained revelry and lechery

save ~ except, but

savest ~ save ~ 3

saveth ~ saves ~ 7

saving ~ excepting, but, *Rare* except

saviour ~ savior ~ 37

saviours ~ saviors ~ 2

savour ~ savor: taste or smell

savourest ~ savor: taste with delight, taste; appreciate

savours ~ savors ~ 1

savoury ~ tasty, flavorful

sawest ~ saw ~ 21

sawn ~ cut

say ~ said

sayest ~ say ~ 40

scaleth ~ scales ~ 1

scall ~ any scaly or scabby skin disease, esp of the scalp

scapegoat ~ object upon which the guilt for others' sins falls

scarce ~ Literary: scarcely; *Arc* scarcely

scarest ~ scare ~ 1

scattereth ~ scatters ~ 10

sceptre ~ scepter ~ 15

schism ~ split or division caused by difference of opinion

schoolmaster ~ *Gk* trusted slave who constantly supervised the life & morals of his master's son until adulthood

science ~ knowledge

scoffers ~ mockers

scorn ~ object of extreme, often indignant, contempt or utter disdain

scorn ~ treat with extreme, often indignant, contempt or utter disdain

scorner ~ one who scorns, derides, or mocks; esp one who scoffs at religion

scorners ~ ones who scorn, deride, or mock; esp ones who scoff at religion

scornest ~ scorn: deride, utterly disdain; mock or scoff at

scorneth ~ scorns: derides, utterly disdains; mocks or scoffs at

scornful ~ full of scorn; derisive; boastful, arrogant

scorning ~ mocking, disdain, scoffing, contempt

scourge ~ whip

scourged ~ whipped

scourgeth ~ scourges: whips, flogs

scourging ~ whipping

scourgings ~ whippings

scrabbled ~ scraped, scratched, or groped about wildly or frantically with the hands.

scribe ~ law-copyist & law-expert

scribes ~ law-copyists; law-experts

scrip ~ *Arc* wallet, small bag, or satchel (*Gk* a leathern sack in which travelers & shepherds carried their provisions; a wallet)

sea ~ i.e. large container for water; the temple's largest laver or water container

sealest ~ seal ~ 1

sealeth ~ seals ~ 3

searchest ~ search ~ 2

searcheth ~ searches ~ 8

seared with a hot iron ~ scorched or burned on the surface; branded, cauterized with a hot iron; made callous or unfeeling; hardened

season ~ time; while; brief time; suitable, proper, fitting, or convenient time; *Gk* little (time)

seasons ~ times

seat ~ thrown-seat

seats ~ *Gk* thrown-seats or chairs of state

sect ~ religious faction or group

secure you ~ protect you; *Gk* free you from anxiety

security of ~ sufficient downpayment or bond from

sedition ~ *Arc* revolt, rebellion

seduce you ~ lead you astray

seducers ~ *Gk* deceivers, impostors

seduceth ~ seduces ~ 1

see to ~ i.e. look upon

seed ~ *Arc* descendants, posterity

seeing then that ~ since

seeing that ~ i.e. since, because; *Gk* since

seeing ~ since, because

seekest ~ seek ~ 9

seeketh ~ seeks ~ 42

seemeth ~ seems ~ 28

seemly ~ fitting, pleasing, proper, becoming, appropriate

seest ~ see ~ 36

seeth ~ sees ~ 54
seethe ~ boil or cook by boiling
seething ~ boiling
selfsame ~ the very same, identical
sellest ~ sell ~ 1
selleth ~ sells ~ 7
selvedge ~ a specially woven edge
that keeps fabric from
unraveling
senate ~ council of elders, Sanhedrin
senators ~ council of elders (*Heb*
elders)
sendest ~ send ~ 6
sendeth ~ sends ~ 15
sentence ~ verdict, judgment,
decision
sentest ~ sent ~ 4
separateth ~ separates ~ 5
sepulchre ~ tomb, grave, burial vault
(Brit spell of sepulcher)
sepulchres ~ tombs, graves, burial
vaults (Brit for sepulchers)
serjeants ~ sergeants, court officers;
(*Gk* lictors, public officials
who bore the fasces or staff
and other insignia of office
before a magistrate)
serpent ~ snake
serpents ~ snakes
served ~ treated
servedst ~ served ~ 1
servest ~ serve ~ 2
serveth ~ serves ~ 9
servile ~ slavish; befitting a slave: i.e.
laborious
servitor ~ servant, attendant
set at liberty ~ released, set free
set at nought ~ *Gk* treated with
contempt, utterly despised;
(*Heb* ne-glected, ignored)
set at nought of ~ *Gk* treated with
contempt by, utterly despised
by

set by ~ i.e. valued
set forth ~ put out; *Gk* set sail, put to
sea
set him at nought ~ i.e. treated him
as if he were nothing (naught);
(*Gk* utterly despised him)
set on ~ attack
set on ~ i.e. serve(d)
set them at one again ~ *Gk* urged
them unto peace
set to ~ *Arc* affixed
set upon ~ i.e. attack
set light by ~ treated with contempt;
dishonored
set your affection ~ *Gk* focus your
mind
set a compass ~ *Arc* traced or
inscribed a circle
set ~ put, placed; i.e. went
setter forth ~ proclaimer
settest ~ set ~ 7
setteth thee on ~ incites, urges you on
setteth light by ~ *Heb* dishonors,
treats with contempt or shame
setteth ~ sets ~ 22
setting a watch ~ i.e. assigning
soldiers to guard
settle ~ *Obs* sitting place, ledge, or
raised platform
settlest ~ settle ~ 1
sevenfold ~ seven times
sever out ~ set apart, separate, or
make a distinction
sever ~ set apart, separate, divide, or
make a distinction
several ~ separate
severally ~ separately, independently
severed ~ separated, or set apart
sewest ~ sew ~ 1
seweth ~ sews ~ 1
shaketh ~ shakes ~ 7
shalt ~ shall ~ 1617

shambles ~ *Rare* place where meat is sold; butcher's stall or shop (Brit)

shamefacedness ~ great modesty, bashfulness, or shyness (*Gk* a sense of shame, modesty, bashfulness)

shameth ~ shames ~ 1

share ~ plow part that cuts the soil: plowshare

sharpeneth ~ sharpens ~ 3

she asses ~ female donkeys, burros

she ~ female

sheaves ~ bundles of harvested grain

shed forth ~ poured out

shed abroad ~ *Gk* poured out

shed ~ poured out

sheddeth ~ sheds ~ 2

sheepcote ~ small shelter or shed for sheep; sheepfold

sheepcotes ~ small shelters or sheds for sheep; sheepfolds

sherd ~ shard--fragment or broken piece, esp of pottery; potsherd

sherds ~ shards--fragments or broken pieces, esp of pottery; potsherds

shew of ~ *Gk* proclaim or declare concerning

shew ~ show; display, declare

shew ~ show: false display, fake performance

shewbread ~ showbread ~ 18

shewed ~ showed: revealed, displayted

shewedst ~ shewed, ~ showed ~ 2

shewest ~ shew, ~ show ~ 5

sheweth ~ shews, ~ shows ~ 20

shewing ~ *Gk* public showing forth

shineth ~ shines ~ 9

shittim ~ an Asiatic acacia with close grained yellowish-brown wood (*Heb* acacia)

Shittim ~ city named for close-grained yellowish-brown wood

shivers ~ fragments, chips, splinters, slivers

shock ~ stacked sheaf

shod ~ shoed: provided with shoes

shoelatchet ~ *Arc* lace or strap that binds a shoe or sandal

shoot forth ~ put out leaves

shooteth ~ shoots ~ 3

shorn ~ cut short the hair of; given a short hair-cut

short space ~ *Gk* little (time)

shouldest ~ should ~ 73

shouteth ~ shouts ~ 1

shroud ~ (*Arc*) cover

shun ~ avoid

shunned ~ hesitated

shut up ~ i.e. imprisoned

shut to ~ *Obs* securely closed or bolted

shutteth ~ shuts ~ 8

sighest ~ sigh ~ 1

sigheth ~ sighs ~ 1

sign ~ authenticating demonstration or miracle

signet ~ seal, esp one used as a signature in marking a document as official; sealing ring

signets ~ seals, esp ones used as a signature in marking a document as official; sealing rings

signified ~ made known by signs or symbols

signifieth ~ signifies ~ 1

signs ~ hand-signals

signs ~ authenticating miracles

silverlings ~ *Arc* shekels (half-ounce Hebrew silver coins)

silversmith ~ artisan who makes or repairs silver objects, esp by shaping the metal while it is hot and soft

similitude ~ likeness, form

similitudes ~ *Obs* allegories, parables, similes

simple ~ someone innocent, easily misled, or ignorant (*Heb* naive, open-minded, foolish)

simplicity ~ generosity; genuineness

sincere ~ without deceit, pretense, or hypocrisy; genuine; *Gk* found pure when unfolded and examined by the sun's light; *Gk* unadulterated, pure

singeth ~ sings ~ 1

single ~ *Gk* sound, healthy

singleness ~ simplicity, sincerity, mental honesty

singular ~ extraordinary

sinnest ~ sin ~ 1

sinneth ~ sins ~ 22

Sion ~ Zion ~ 9

sith ~ *Arc* since

sittest ~ sit ~ 7

sitteth ~ sits ~ 42

situate ~ *Arc* situated: placed, located

situation ~ location, position

sixscore ~ one hundred twenty (a score=20)

skippedst ~ skipped ~ 1

skirt ~ i.e. bottom part

slack ~ delay, hesitate, be slow; relax, delay, slow

slack ~ slow; negligent; idle; hesitant; sluggish, loose

slackness ~ slowness, sluggishness; delay

slain ~ kill(ed) or destroyed in a violent way; kill (i.e. animals for food)

slanderest ~ slander ~ 1

slandereth ~ slanders ~ 1

slayeth ~ slays: kills or destroys in a violent way

slaying ~ killing or destroying in a violent way

sleep ~ i.e. are dead

sleepest ~ sleep ~ 4

sleepeth ~ sleeps ~ 7

sleight ~ cunning or craft used in deception

slept ~ i.e. died

slew ~ kill(ed) or destroy(ed) in a violent way

slewest ~ slew, ~ killed ~ 1

slideth ~ slides ~ 1

slime ~ pitch, bitumen, asphalt

slimepits ~ pits or holes yielding asphalt or bitumen

slippeth ~ slips ~ 3

slips ~ stems, roots, twigs, etc. cut or broken off a plant and used for planting or grafting; cuttings, scions

slothful ~ sluggish, slow, lazy, inactive

slothfulness ~ sluggishness, laziness, inactivity

slow bellies ~ i.e. lazy gluttons

sluggard ~ habitually lazy or idle person

sluices ~ artificial channels or passages for water, having a gate or valve at their heads to regulate the flow

slumbereth ~ slumbers: sleeps

smart ~ suffer pain

smelleth ~ smells ~ 1

smite out ~ knock out

smite ~ *Rare* strike or hit hard; attack; destroy; kill

smitest ~ smite: hit or strike hard

smiteth through ~ *Rare* hits or strikes hard; attacks; destroys; kills

smiteth ~ smites: *Rare* hits or strikes hard; attacks; destroys; kills

smith ~ person who makes or repairs metal objects, esp by shaping metal while it is hot & soft; metalworker

smiting ~ *Rare* striking or hitting hard; attacking; destroying; killing

smitten ~ *Rare* struck or hit hard; attacked; destroyed; killed

smootheth ~ smoothes ~ 1

smote ~ *Rare* struck or hit hard; destroyed; killed

smotest ~ smote: *Rare* struck, hit hard

snare ~ noose-like trap for catching small animals

snared ~ caught in a noose-like trap used for small animals

snares ~ noose-like traps for small animals

snuffed ~ sniffed

snuffeth ~ snuffs: sniffs

so much the more ~ i.e. even more

sobriety ~ *Gk* self-control; a sound mind

sod ~ boiled

sodden ~ boiled

sodoma ~ i.e. Sodom

sodomite ~ a person who practices sodomy--any sexual intercourse held to be abnormal, esp anal intercourse between two male persons or bestiality (*Heb* a male temple prostitute)

sodomites ~ persons who practice sodomy--any sexual intercourse held to be abnormal, esp anal intercourse between two male persons or bestiality (*Heb* male temple prostitutes)

soever ~ i.e. whatever

sojourn ~ stay, dwell, or live temporarily

sojourned ~ stayed, dwelt, or lived temporarily

sojourner ~ visitor, temporary resident

sojourneth ~ sojourns: stays, dwells, or lives temporarily

sojourning ~ temporarily stay or staying temporarily

solace ~ comfort, soothe, console, relieve

solemnity ~ solemn ceremony, ritual

solitary ~ lonely, isolated, alone

some time ~ *Arc* formerly

sometime ~ *Arc* formerly

sometimes ~ *Arc* formerly; *Gk* once, formerly

somewhat ~ i.e. something, anything

somewhat ~ to some degree or extent; a little

soothsayer ~ one who professes to foretell the future

soothsayers ~ ones who profess to foretell the future

soothsaying ~ making predictions

sop ~ piece of bread dipped in liquid before eating

sorcerers ~ wizards

sorceries ~ magic arts, witchcraft; black magic; witchery

sore ~ *Heb* plague spot, plague, disease, stroke

sore ~ *Arc* exceedingly great, severe; greatly, extremely, exceedingly, greatly

sorely ~ *Arc* severely, greatly

sorer ~ *Arc* greater, worse

sorroweth ~ sorrows ~ 1

sottish ~ like a sot (drunkard): stupid or foolish as from too much drinking
sound ~ healthy
sounded ~ probed the depths of, i.e. thoroughly questioned
sounded ~ measured water depth
soundeth ~ sounds ~ 1
sow ~ female pig
sowedst ~ sowed ~ 1
sowest ~ sow ~ 3
soweth ~ sows ~ 15
space ~ time
spake ~ spoke ~ 598
spakest ~ spake, ~ spoke ~ 10
span ~ distance from extended pinky to thumb; i.e. about nine inches
spareth ~ spares ~ 4
sparingly ~ in a stingy, sparing manner
speakest ~ speak ~ 17
speaketh ~ speaks ~ 74
specially ~ *Obs* especially
speed ~ success, fortune
spendest ~ spend ~ 1
spendeth ~ spends ~ 3
spent ~ used up
spied ~ saw, observed; seen
spikenard ~ very fragrant ointment or oil derived from the head or spike of the nard plant; liquid or pure nard
spitefully entreated ~ shamefully or maliciously *Arc* treated
spitefully ~ shamefully
spittle ~ spit, saliva
spoil ~ plundering, looting; *Heb* devastation, ruin
spoil ~ goods or territory taken by force in war; plunder; devastation, ruin

spoil ~ take goods by force in war, plunder, loot;
spoiled ~ ruined; *Arc* robbed, pillaged, plundered, looted
spoilers ~ plunderers, looters, pillagers; robbers
spoilest ~ spoil ~ 1
spoileth ~ spoils: takes goods by force in war, plunders, loots
spoiling ~ taking goods by force in war, plundering, looting
spoils ~ goods taken in battle, plunder
sporting themselves with ~ reveling or delighting in
sporting ~ (amorously) playing or frolicking,
spreadest ~ spread ~ 1
spreadeth ~ spreads ~ 14
spreading ~ scattering, dispersing
springeth ~ springs ~ 4
springs ~ sources, origins, motives
sprinkleth ~ sprinkles ~ 2
spue ~ spew: vomit
spued ~ spewed ~ 1
spy out ~ i.e. view
stablish ~ *Arc* establish: make stable, firm; strengthen, settle, confirm, stabilize; fulfill; cause to happen
stablished ~ *Arc* established: settled
stablisheth ~ stablishes: *Arc* establishes
staggereth ~ staggers ~ 1
stanched ~ stopped (mod sp staunched)
stand to it ~ i.e. stands firm
standard ~ flag or banner
standards ~ flags or banners
standest ~ stand ~ 6
standeth ~ stands ~ 30
stank ~ stunk, i.e. were very offensive
state ~ condition

stature ~ height
staves ~ staffs: poles (alt pl)
stay ~ support; wait, i.e. delay; stop,
    i.e. standstill
stay ~ restrain, hold back, remain,
    refrain; hinder ; wait, i.e.
    delay; stop, i.e. standstill;
    (*Heb* make to lie down); rely;
    support, sustain, supply
stayed ~ fixed
stayed ~ halted, stopped; held back;
    propped; restrained, detained;
    remained; remained, relied,
    leaned; waited
stayeth ~ stays: stops, restrains
stays ~ supports
stead ~ place
steads ~ places
stealeth ~ steals ~ 3
stedfast ~ firmly fixed; steadfastly:
    firmly, strongly
stedfastly ~ unwaveringly, constantly
stedfastness ~ firmness of belief
steemeth ~ considers, judges
steppeth ~ steps ~ 1
steward ~ estate or household
    manager
stewards ~ managers of a large estate
sticketh ~ sticks ~ 1
still ~ silent, quiet; silence
stilled ~ quieted
stillest ~still: quiet, calm
stilleth ~ stills: quiets
stingeth ~ stings ~ 1
stinketh ~ stinks ~ 2
stir ~ disturbance; commotion,
    agitation
stirreth ~ stirs ~ 8
stirs ~ shakings, agitations; *Heb*
    noises
stock ~ *Arc* wooden block or log
stock ~ lineage, family

stocks ~ blocks of wood, logs
stomacher ~ richly ornamented,
    triangular piece of cloth
    formerly worn, esp by women
    as a covering for the chest or
    abdomen
stones ~ *Arc* testicles
stonest ~ stone ~ 2
stoodest ~ stood ~ 3
stoopeth ~ stoops ~ 1
stopped ~ closed up; muzzled; shut;
    blocked
stoppeth ~ stops ~ 4
store to ~ supply or reserve for
store ~ storage, reserve; abundance;
    supply
stories ~ (heavenly) *Heb* steps, stairs,
    levels
stout ~ forceful, powerful
straightway ~ immediately
strait ~ *Arc* narrow or confining;
    narrow place--i.e. difficulty or
    difficult
straiten them ~ *Arc* restrict them
    closely, hem them in
straitened ~ *Arc* closely restricted,
    hemmed in
straiteneth ~ *Arc* narrows, restricts
straiteneth ~ straitens ~ 1
straitest ~ *Arc* strictest
straitly ~ *Arc* strictly, urgently
straitness ~ *Arc* distress, confinement
straits ~ *Arc* narrows or narrow
    places--i.e. difficulties
strake sail ~ lowered the sail
strakes ~ *Arc* streaks; strips; stripes
strange ~ foreign, alien
strawed ~ *Arc* strewed--scattered
strengthenedst ~ strengthened ~ 1
strengtheneth ~ strengthens ~ 7
stretchedst ~ stretched ~ 1
stretchest ~ stretch ~ 1

stretcheth ~ stretches ~ 7
stricken in ~ struck by : i.e. along in
strife ~ conflict: quarrel, dispute,
     struggle; *Gk* contradiction,
     opposition
strifes of words ~ word-battles
strifes ~ fights
striker ~ striking or punching addict
striketh ~ strikes ~ 3
stripes ~ whip-strokes, long skin-
     welts; blood-trickling wounds;
     Arc strokes with a whip; long
     welts on the skin; lashes of a
     whip; welts
stripling ~ one as thin as a strip:
     youth, young person
stript ~ stripped ~ 1
strive ~ fight, struggle; argue, debate;
     compete
strived ~ struggled, agonized, fought
striveth ~ strives ~ 2
striving ~ struggling, battles
strove ~ contended, struggled; fought;
     Obs vied
strowed ~ *Arc* strewed--scattered
stubble ~ short stumps of grain left
     standing
studieth ~ studies: ponders; tries hard
study ~ try hard; *Gk* be diligent
stuff ~ household or personal
     possessions; household goods,
     belongings
stumbleth ~ stumbles ~ 4
subduedst ~ subdued ~ 1
subdueth ~ subdues ~ 3
subject unto ~ submissive to, under
     the authority of
subject to like passions ~ *Gk* of
     similar feelings
subject ~ submissive, obedient; being
     subjected, submitting

subjection ~ *Obs* obedience,
     submission; *Gk* slavery: stern,
     rigid discipline
submit ~ under-rank; subordinate
suborned ~ bribed
substance ~ wealth, property,
     possessions
subtil ~ subtle: crafty, sly
subtilly ~ *Rare* spell of subtilely:
     craftily, slyly
subtilty ~ craftiness, deceit, guile,
     trickery; deception; (*Rare*
     spell)
suburbs ~ areas located just outside
     of a city
subvert ~ overturn, corrupt
subverted ~ turned inside out,
     corrupted
succeedest ~ succeed ~ 2
succour ~ succor: help, aid, rescue in
     time of need
succoured ~ succored: helped, aided,
     rescued in time of need
succourer ~ succorer: helper (in time
     of need)
such like ~ suchlike: similar, in like
     manner; of such a kind
suckling ~ unweaned or nursing child
sucklings ~ unweaned or nursing
     children
suffer ~ endure, permit, allow,
     tolerate, put up with; let;
     experience
suffer ~ permit, allow
suffered ~ permitted, tolerated;
     experienced, endured;
     allowed; let
sufferest ~ suffer: tolerate, permit,
     allow
suffereth long ~ endures for a long
     time

suffereth ~ suffers: experiences; endures; permits

suffice ~ *Arc* satisfy, be enough for

sufficed **them** **not** ~ i.e. were not enough

sufficed ~ satisfied

sufficeth ~ suffices: *Arc* satisfies

sufficient **unto** ~ enough for

sum ~ total, count; i.e. summary

sunder ~ pieces, parts

sundered ~ separated, split apart

sundry ~ various, diverse

sup up ~ eat the evening meal; have supper; gobble up

sup ~ eat the evening meal; have supper

superfluity ~ overflowing, superabundance

superfluous ~ unnecessary, not needed

superscription ~ inscription or engraving on top or outer surface; surface inscription; *Gk* inscription, title

supped ~ eaten the evening meal

supplant ~ take the place of through force or plotting

supplanted ~ uprooted, replaced, esp through treachery

supple ~ soften

suppliants ~ petitioners

supplication ~ humble request, prayer, petition, pea

supplications ~ humble requests, petitions, or pleas

supplieth ~ supplies ~ 2

sure ~ certain, secure, firm

surely ~ certainly

surety ~ certainty; one responsible for another's debts; legally responsible; contract

surfeiting ~ overindulgence, gluttony, excess

surmisings ~ conjectures, guesses

surname ~ other name; nickname; i.e. also named; *Obs* second or other name

sustenance ~ nourishment, food

swaddled ~ swathed, bound, or wrapped with strips of cloth

swaddling **clothes** ~ long, narrow bands of cloth wrapped around a newborn in former times

swaddlingband ~ swathing, wrapping cloth or band

swalloweth ~ swallows ~ 2

swarest ~ sware, ~ swore ~ 5

sweareth ~ swears ~ 11

swelling ~ arrogant, prideful

swellings ~ arrogance, pride

swimmest ~ swim ~ 1

swimmeth ~ swims ~ 1

swine ~ pigs

sworn ~ promised with an oath to

sycamine ~ mulberry tree

sycomore ~ sycamore ~ 7

Syriack ~ Aramaic

Syrian ~ Aramaic

tabering ~ beating of a drum

tabernacle ~ *Arc* temporary shelter, tent

tabernacles ~ *Arc* temporary shelters, tents

tables ~ thin, flat tablets used for inscriptions

tables ~ tablets; small flat things to wear as an ornament

tabret ~ small drum

tabrets ~ small drums

taches ~ *Arc* devices for fastening two parts together, fasteners: clasps, buckles, hooks

take account ~ settle accounts

take care for ~ worry, concern himself about

take heed ~ pay close attention to; listen carefully; beware

take no thought ~ *Gk* do not worry or be anxious; *Gk* stop worrying

take ye thought ~ *Gk* worry or be anxious; do ye worry

taken our leave one of ~ said good-by to one

takest ~ take ~ 9

taketh ~ takes: grasps, captures

taking my leave of ~ saying farewell to

taking thought ~ *Gk* worrying

tale ~ *Arc* tally, count, enumeration

talebearer ~ gossip, slanderer

talents ~ talent=large unit of weight or money; *Gk* In Israel, a talent of silver weighed about 100 pounds (45 kg); and a talent of gold weighed about 200 pounds (91 kg).

talkest ~ talk ~ 3

talketh ~ talks ~ 2

tare ~ tore

tares ~ vetch, darnel, or weeds in general

target ~ small shield, esp a round one; buckler

targets ~ small shields, esp a round ones; bucklers

tarried ~ remained, stayed, waited; delayed (his arrival)

tarriest ~ tarry: wait

tarrieth ~ tarries ~ 2

tarry ~ remain temporarily, remain for a time; remain, wait, delay, hesitate, linger

tarry abroad ~ i.e. remain outdoors, or outside

tarrying ~ delay

tasteth ~ tastes ~ 1

tattlers ~ gossips

taught ~ i.e. instructed

taxing ~ *Gk* registration, census (for taxing purposes)

teachest ~ teach ~ 8

teacheth ~ teaches ~ 16

teareth ~ tears ~ 6

teats ~ nipples

tedious ~ long-winded, boring

teil ~ linden or lime tree

tell ~ count, enumerate, reckon

tellest ~ tell ~ 1

telleth ~ tells: *Arc* counts

temper ~ *Arc* mix (in proper proportions)

temperance ~ self-control; self-restraint

temperate ~ self-controlled; self-restrained

tempered ~ *Arc* mixed (in proper proportions)

tempest ~ violent storm with strong winds

tempestuous ~ stormy, violent

temporal ~ temporary

tempt ~ test or try

temptation ~ testing, trial

temptations ~ testings or trials of any kind

tempted ~ tested, put to the test, tried

tempted of ~ tested, tried by

tempteth ~ tempts ~ 1

tempting ~ testing

tendeth ~ tends ~ 5

tenons ~ projections on the end or side of wood that fit into corresponding holes or cavities in another place

tenor ~ general tendency or meaning

teraphim ~ small images or other things representing household gods, used among ancient Semitic peoples: idols

terrestrial ~ earthly, worldly

terrible ~ fear-producing, fearful, awe-inspiring, terror-inspiring, terror-causing, terror-producing, terrifying

terrifiest ~ terrify ~ 1

testament ~ covenant (esp between God and man); *Rare* will

testator ~ person who has drawn up a will

testifiedst ~ testified ~ 2

testifieth ~ testifies ~ 5

tetrarch ~ ruler of part (one fourth) of a Roman province

thank ~ thanks, reward

thankworthy ~ worthy of thanks, commendable

that ~ i.e. what; i.e. also; *Gk* this that; *Gk* what or that

that thine is ~ i.e. what is thine

the deep ~ Poetic: the sea or the ocean

the dropsy ~ *Obs* edema: fluid over-accumulation

the even ~ *Arc* the evening

the transgression of the law ~ lawlessness

the ministry ~ *Gk* service

the more ~ i.e. even more; to a greater degree

the more carefully ~ *Gk* speedily, hastily, diligently

the more silence ~ i.e. even more silent

the multitude ~ a host, great number

the preeminence ~ the surpassing excellence; *Gk* first place

thee ~ you (singular) ~ 3826-

thee-ward ~toward you (singular) ~ 1-

theeward ~ toward you (singular)

thence ~ *Arc* there; (from) that place or time

thenceforth ~ from that time onward; after that; thereafter

thenceforth ~ therefore

thereabout ~ about this

thereat ~ there; at that place or time

thereby ~ by this or by it

therefore ~ therefore; for this reason; for which cause; *Arc* why?

therefrom ~ from it; from them

therein ~ in there, in it, in them

thereinto ~ into it

thereof ~ of it

thereon ~ on it; on that

thereout ~ out of it

thereto ~ to it

thereunto ~ unto it

thereupon ~ upon it

therewith ~ with it, with which, with them

thicket ~ thick growth of shrubs

thine ~ your (singular) ~ 937 ~ yours (singular) ~ 21-

thinkest ~ think ~ 9

thinketh ~ thinks ~ 6

thirsteth ~ thirsts ~ 4

thirtyfold ~ thirty times (as much)

this wise ~ this way

thither ~ there; to or toward that place

thitherward ~ *Rare* toward that place; there

thongs ~ leather straps

thou ~ you (singular) ~ 5473-

thought ~ thought [it]

thought scorn ~ rejected as disgraceful; utterly disdained

thoughtest ~ thought ~ 1

thoughts ~ *Gk* doubts, hesitations

threescore ~ sixty (a score=20)

thresheth ~ threshes ~ 1
threwest ~ threw ~ 1
thrice ~ three times
throng ~ crowd or press upon in large
    numbers
thronged ~ pressed against
thronging ~ pressing against
throughly ~ *Arc* completely
throughly furnished ~ completely
    equipped
throughly purge ~ completely
    cleanse
thrust in ~ *Gk* drive, propel
thrusteth ~ thrusts ~ 1
thundereth ~ thunders ~ 3
thus.~ in this manner
thy ~ your (singular) ~ 4603-
thyine ~ the citrus, an odoriferous
    North African tree used as
    incense, prized by the ancient
    Greeks and Romans on
    account of the beauty of its
    wood for various ornamental
    purposes
thyself ~ yourself ~ 215-
tidings ~ news
till ~ until
till ~ cultivate
tillage ~ cultivating of land to raise
    crops, as by plowing,
    fertilizing etc.; land that is
    cultivated
tillest ~ till: cultivate
tilleth ~ tills ~ 2
timbrel ~ ancient type of tambourine
    or drum
timbrels ~ ancient type of
    tambourines or drums
time ~ i.e. delay
times ~ i.e. periods of time
Ttimotheus ~ Timothy ~ 19
tire ~ *Arc* attire: head-dress, turban

tired her head ~ attired her head, i.e.
    arranged her hair
tires ~ *Arc* attires: head-dresses
tithes ~ tenth portions or parts
title ~ *Obs* inscription on a sign or
    placard
tittle ~ small pen-stroke (*Gk* "little
    horn"--used by grammarians
    of the accents and diacritical
    points. Jesus used it of the
    little lines or projections, by
    which the Hebrew letters in
    other respects similar differ
    from one another; the meaning
    is, "not even the minutest part
    of the law shall perish".)
to ~ i.e. as his; i.e. to be his; i.e. as;
    i.e. [something] to
to and fro ~ back and forth
to edification ~ *Gk* towards building
    up
to God-ward ~ *Arc* toward God
to morrow ~ tomorrow
to pledge ~ i.e. as a down-payment or
    collateral
to the intent ~ i.e. so that; *Gk* so that,
    in order that
to the intent that ~ *Gk* so that, in
    order that
to the mercy seatward ~ toward the
    mercy seat
to the spoil ~ i.e. as goods or territory
    taken by force in war
to their minister ~ for or as their
    assistant, attendant
to us-ward ~ *Arc* toward us
to wit ~ *Arc* that is to say, namely; for
    example
to you-ward ~ *Arc* toward you
    (plural)

token ~ sign or symbol (of genuineness, assurance, or authority)

tokens ~ signs or symbols (of genuineness, assurance, or authority)

told ~ counted, enumerated, reckoned

took ~ mistook

took ~ boarded a; *Gk* stepped or went into a

took his leave of ~ said good-by to

took knowledge of ~ recognized

took shipping ~ *Gk* got into boats

took to wife ~ i.e. married

tookest ~ took ~ 2

torment ~ torture

tormented ~ tortured

tormentors ~ *Gk* torturers

torments ~ tortures

tottering ~ unstable, unsteady

toucheth ~ touches ~ 40

touching ~ concerning, with regard to

tow ~ the coarse and broken fibers of flax, hemp, etc. prepared for spinning

toward ~ favorable towards

traffick ~ traffic: trade (*Arc* sp)

traffickers ~ traffickers: traders

train ~ caravan

transfigured ~ transformed, metamorphosized

transgress ~ overstep, break

transgressest ~ transgress ~ 1

transgresseth the law ~ practices lawlessness

transgresseth ~ transgresses ~ 4

transgressor ~ lawbreaker

translate ~ transfer or transport: move from place or condition to another

translated ~ transferred or transported: moved from one place or condition to another

translation ~ transfer or transport: move from one place or condition to another

travail ~ toil, work very hard; painfully labor; agonize; sudden, sharp, and brief pains--physical or emotional; spasms of distress; labor pains, pains of childbirth; agony, intense pain

travail with child ~ experience labor-pains

travailed ~ toiled, worked very hard: went into labor, began to give birth

travailest ~ travail: labors in birth (*Gk* feels childbirth's labor/ pain)

travaileth ~ travails ~ 7

travaileth ~ toils, works very hard: experiences labor pains

travailing ~ birth-giving, laboring (with the birth process)

travelled ~ traveled

traveller ~ traveler

travelleth ~ travels ~ 2

travelling ~ traveling

tread ~ walk, trample

treadeth ~ treads: tramples, threshes

treasurest ~ treasure ~ 1

treatise ~ *Obs* narrative

tree ~ i.e. cross

trembleth ~ trembles ~ 4

trespass ~ do wrong; cross the line, sin; go beyond the limits of justice or morality

tresspass ~ going beyond the limits of justice or morality

trial ~ *Obs* experience

tribulation ~ great misery or distress; affliction; oppression, suffering

tribulations ~ great miseries or distresses; afflictions, sufferings

tributaries ~ forced laborers; subject nations

tributary ~ under the control of another nation

tribute ~ forced service or required payment; tax levied on a conquered nation; subject-nation tax; i.e. "contribution"

trickleth ~ trickles ~ 1

triest ~ try ~ 3

trieth ~ tries ~ 5

trimmest ~ trim ~ 1

trodden ~ trampled

trode ~ trampled

troop ~ group or body of soldiers

troubledst ~ troubled ~ 1

troublest ~ trouble ~ 1

troubleth ~ troubles ~ 10

trow ~ *Arc* think, suppose, believe

trump ~ trumpet

trustedst ~ trusted ~ 3

trustest ~ trust ~ 6

trusteth ~ trusts ~ 3

tumult ~ uproar, noisy commotion; loud noise, din; noisy confusion

tumults ~ uproars, noisy commotions

turn ~ return

turnest ~ turn ~ 3

turneth ~ turns ~ 33

turtle ~ *Arc* turtledove

turtles ~ *Arc* for turtledoves

tutors ~ legal guardians (*Gk* ones who have the care & tutelage of children whether father be dead or alive)

twain ~ two (*Arc* variant)

twined ~ intertwined, woven, twisted, interlaced

unawares ~ unintentionally, without knowing or being aware; unexpectedly, suddenly, by surprise

unblameable **and** **unreproveable** ~ *Gk* without blemish & blame

uncomely ~ unattractive; unbecoming; improper (*Gk* deformed; unseemly, indecent)

uncovereth ~ uncovers ~ 3

unction ~ anointing

under **colour** ~ i.e. pretending

undersetters ~ supports, bases (*Obs*)

understandest ~ understand ~ 4

understandeth ~ understands ~ 11

undressed ~ unattended, not cultivated

unfeigned ~ genuine, real; sincere

ungirded ~ unbound, unloaded

unicorn ~ *Obs* one-horned rhinoceros: used in the Middle English O.T. to render the Latin Vulgate unicornis or rhinoceros and retained in later versions (*Heb* probably the great aurochs or wild bulls which are now extinct. The exact meaning is not known.)

unicorns ~ *Obs* one-horned rhinoceroses: used in the Middle English O.T. to render the Latin Vulgate unicornis or rhinoceros and retained in later versions (*Heb* probably the great aurochs or wild bulls which are now extinct. The exact meaning is not known.)

unlade ~ unload, unburden (Rare)

unquenchable ~ that can not be put out or extinguished

unruly ~ not subject to rules; unrestrained

unsatiable ~ insatiable: not able to be satisfied

unsearchable ~ incomprehensible

unseemly ~ indecent or improper; indecently or improperly

unshod ~ without shoes; barefooted

unspeakable ~ indescribable, description-defying

untempered ~ *Arc* unmixed (in proper proportions)

untimely birth ~ premature birth, miscarriage

untimely ~ premature: unripe

unto ~ to [in the view of]; *Gk* until

untoward ~ *Arc* stubborn, unruly

unwashen ~ unwashed

unwittingly ~ unknowingly

up ~ i.e. get up; i.e. go up

upbraid ~ rebuke severely or bitterly; censure sharply; scold

upbraided ~ rebuked severely or bitterly; censured sharply; scolded

upbraideth ~ upbraids: rebukes severely or bitterly; censures sharply; scolds

upholdest ~ uphold ~ 1

upholdeth ~ upholds ~ 4

uppermost rooms ~ most prestigious places

urgent ~ insistent

used ~ (mis)treated

used to push ~ i.e. often tried to gore

usest ~ use ~ 1

useth ~ uses ~ 7

usurer ~ one who lends at (excessively high) interest

usurp ~ unjustly take or assume

usury ~ lending at (excessively high) interest; loans at (excessively high) interest; (excessively high) interest

utmost ~ outermost, farthest

utter ~ complete, total; absolute

utter ~ outer, outward, external

utter ~ speak, tell; make known;

utterance ~ words, speech; *Gk* logos: discourse, speech, words

uttereth ~ utters ~ 9

utterly ~ completely, totally

uttermost ~ outermost, farthest, most distant or remote

vagabond ~ wandering, vagrant, shiftless

vagabond ~ wanderer, vagrant, nomad, drifter, tramp

vagabonds ~ wanderers, vagrants, transients, drifters

vail ~ veil: curtain

vain ~ empty, worthless, futile; useless

vain jangling ~ foolish, idle, annoying, angry, or meaningless talk

vainglory ~ extreme self-pride and boastfulness; excessive & ostentatious vanity

vale ~ valley (Poetic)

valiant ~ courageous, brave; strong

valour ~ valor: courage, boldness, bravery

valuest ~ value ~ 1

vanisheth ~ vanishes ~ 2

vanities ~ things vain, futile, idle, or worthless

vanity ~ futility, idleness, or worthlessness; emptiness; something truly vain, futile, idle, or worthless

vapour ~ vapor ~ 5

vapours ~ vapors ~ 3

variableness ~ variation, change

vaunt ~ boast or brag
vaunteth ~ vaunts ~ 1
vehement ~ strong, ardent, vigorous, intense
vehemently ~ strongly, ardently, vigorously, intensely
veil ~ curtain
vein ~ Geology. A regularly shaped and lengthy occurrence of an ore; a lode
vengeance ~ revenge, punishment; avenging justice
venison ~ *Obs* flesh of a game animal used as food
verily ~ *Arc* truly, in very truth
verity ~ truth
vermilion ~ bright red mercuric sulfide used as a pigment: bright red or scarlet color
very chiefest ~ i.e. most important
vessel ~ container; *Obs* body
vestments ~ gowns, robes (esp those used ceremonially)
vestry ~ room for storing or putting on vestments
vesture ~ *Rare* clothing, garment, apparel
vex ~ trouble, disturb; distress, afflict
vexation ~ trouble, distress
vexations ~ troubles, distresses
vexed ~ troubled, disturbed; distressed, afflicted
vial ~ small container for liquids: (*Heb* flask; *Gk* broad, shallow bowl)
vials ~ small containers for liquids; *Gk* shallow bowl(s)
victual ~ food or provisions
victuals ~ articles of food; supplies, sustenance, provisions
vigilant ~ watchful, alert

vile ~ morally base or evil, wicked, depraved, sinful; repulsive disgusting; degrading, base
vilely ~ in a manner morally base or evil, wicked, depraved, sinful; repulsive disgusting; degrading
viler ~ more morally base or evil, wicked, depraved, sinful; repulsive disgusting; degrading
vilest ~ most morally base or evil, wicked, depraved
villany ~ villainy: wicked, detestable, or disgraceful things
vintage ~ grape gathering or time of grape gathering
viol ~ any of an early family of stringed instruments used chiefly in 15th & 16th centuries in sizes from bass viol to treble viol (akin to base fiddle & violin)
viols ~ any of an early family of stringed instruments used chiefly in the 15th & 16th centuries in sizes from bass viol to treble viol (akin to base fiddle & violin)
viper ~ poisonous snake
vipers ~ poisonous snakes
virtue ~ moral excellence: chastity, merit, valor; effective power or force, esp the power to heal or strengthen
visage ~ countenance, face, expression; appearance
visit ~ bring reward, aid, or assistance; inflict punishment, suffering, or judgment (to)
visitation ~ esp, the bringing of punishment, suffering, or judgment, as by God; the

bringing of reward, aid, or assistance

visited ~

visited ~ inflicted punishment, suffering, or judgment; brought reward, aid, or assistance to·

visited me ~ brought me aid or comfort

visitest ~visit: bring reward, aid, or assistance unto

visiteth ~ visits: inflicts punishment, suffering, or judgment

visiting ~ bringing or inflicting punishment, suffering, or judgment upon

vocation ~ calling

void ~ empty; useless, ineffective; invalid; useless, ineffective

volume ~ scroll, roll

vomiteth ~ vomits ~ 1

vowedst ~ vowed ~ 1

vowest ~ vow ~ 2

voweth ~ vows ~ 1

wail ~ *Gk* beat their breasts for grief

waiteth ~ waits ~ 11

wakeneth ~ wakens ~ 2

waketh ~ wakes ~ 2

walkedst ~ walked ~ 1

walkest ~ walk ~ 7

walkest orderly ~ *Gk* march in step

walketh ~ walks ~ 41

wanderest ~ wander ~ 1

wandereth ~ wanders ~ 6

want ~ lack, need

wanted ~ lacked, needed

wanteth ~ wants: lacks, needs

wanting ~ lacking, needing; i.e. missing

wanton ~ sexually loose or unrestrained; recklessly or arrogantly ignoring justice,

decency, morality, etc.; un-disciplined, unmanageable

wantonness ~ *Gk* unbridled lust, licentiousness, lasciviousness, shamelessness

wants ~ lacks, needs

ward ~ guard, custody, watch; custody, guardianship, confinement; *Arc* garrison, guard, watch

ward ~ guard house, jail, prison

wards ~ *Arc* watches i.e. shifts

ware ~ wore

ware ~ *Arc* of aware: cautious

ware ~ wares, goods, merchandise

wares ~ goods, merchandise

warmeth ~ warms ~ 2

warp ~ weaving term: the threads running lengthwise in the loom and crossed by the weft or woof

warreth ~ wars ~ 1

was set ~ i.e. had sat

was forward ~ *Gk* endeavored, gave diligence, made haste

washest ~ wash

wast ~ were ~ 66

waste ~ wild; ruined

waste ~ destroy; wear out; ruin, devastate

wasted ~ devastated, ruined

wastes ~ ruins, destroyed places

wasteth ~ wastes: ruins, devastates, destroys

wasting ~ devastation, ruin

watcheth ~ watches ~ 3

watchings ~ vigils, sleepless watchings

wateredst ~ watered ~ 1

waterest ~ water ~ 2

watereth ~ waters ~ 5

wavereth ~ wavers ~ 1

wax ~ grow, become

waxed ~ grew, became; grown, become

waxen ~ grown, become

waxeth ~ waxes: grows, becomes

waxing ~ growing, becoming

wayfaring ~ traveling, wandering

waymarks ~ road markers

ways ~ roads, paths

weakeneth ~ weakens ~ 2

wealth ~ *Obs* well-being; prosperity

weareth ~ wears ~ 1

wearieth ~ wearies ~ 2

weavest ~ weave ~ 1

weepest ~ weep ~ 3

weepeth ~ weeps ~ 4

weigheth ~ weighs ~ 2

welfare ~ well-being

wench ~ girl, maid-servant, young woman

went about ~ went or walked around

went a whoring ~ prostituted themselves: lit. through cult prostitution to false gods or fig. By spiritual unfaithfulness to the true God

wentest ~ went ~ 14

wert ~ were ~ 6

what thing soever ~ whatever thing

what supplication soever ~ whatever supplication

what saddle soever ~ whatever saddle

what prayer and supplication soever ~ whatever prayer and supplication

what place soever ~ whatever place

what things soever ~ whatever things

what wilt thou ~ will you (have): i.e. what do you want

what man soever ~ whatever man

what cause soever ~ whatever cause

what ~ who

what do ye ~ what are you (pl) doing?

whatsoever ~ whatever

wheaten ~ wheat

whelp ~ cub

whelps ~ cubs

whence ~ (from) where, (from) what place; where

whensoever ~ whenever (emphatic)

whereabout ~ *Obs* on which, about which

whereas ~ i.e. on the contrary, on the other hand; i.e. while; i.e. although, in reality

whereby ~ by which; *Arc* by what? How?

wherefore ~ therefore; for which cause, for this cause; *Arc* why?

wherein ~ in which; i.e. (in those things) in which; *Arc* how? In what way?

whereinsoever ~ *Obs* in whatever (way)

whereinto ~ into which

whereinto ~ where to ~ into which ~ 3-

whereof ~ of what, which, whom; (something) of which

whereon ~ on which; *Arc* on what?

wheresoever ~ wherever (emphatic); at, in, or to whatever place

whereto ~ to which; to what?

whereunto ~ *Arc* of whereto: toward what end or direction; unto which; unto what?

whereupon ~ upon which, upon what; at which, because of which

wherewith ~ with which; that with which; *Arc* with what?

wherewithal ~ *Arc* of wherewith--*Arc* with what?

whet ~ sharpen, hone

whether ~ *Obs* if; whether or not; *Arc* which (of two)?

whiles ~ *Obs* while

whilst ~ *Obs* while

whirleth ~ whirls ~ 1

whisperer ~ slanderer, backbiter

whit ~ bit (small amount)

white ~ whiten

whited ~ whitewashed

whither ~ where, to what place

whithersoever ~ *Arc* of wheresoever: wherever (emphatic): to whatever place

whole ~ healthy. in health

wholly ~ completely, entirely

whomsoever ~ whomever (emphatic)

whore ~ prostitute, harlot; female engaging in promiscuous sexual intercourse: slut

whoredom ~ prostitution, fornication; fig. Being false to God, idolatry

whoremonger ~ man who has sexual intercourse with or associates with whores; fornicator, lecher (*Gk* male prostitute; fornicator)

whoremongers ~ men who have sexual intercourse with or associate with whores; fornicators, lechers (*Gk* male prostitutes; fornicators)

whores ~ prostitutes, harlots; promiscuous females, sluts

whoring ~ prostituted themselves (there): lit. through cult prostitution to false gods or fig. by spiritual unfaith-fulness to the true God

whorish ~ whore-like, lewd

whose soever ~ whoevers'

whose sign was ~ marked by the image of

whoso ~ *Arc* whoever (short for whosoever)

whosoever ~ whoever (emphatic)

wicked ~ wicked (one)

wiles ~ sly tricks; clever schemes

wilily ~ slyly, craftily, deceitfully

will ~ wish, want; *Gk* will to

willeth ~ wills ~ 1

wilt thou ~ i.e. do you want or wish

wilt ~ will, wish

wimples ~ folded garments worn by women to cover the head and neck (*Heb* cloaks)

winebibber ~ drunkard, wino

winebibbers ~ drunkards, winos

winefat ~ *Arc* wine vat, wine press

winketh ~ winks ~ 2

winneth ~ wins ~ 1

winnoweth ~ winnows ~ 1

winnoweth ~ separates chaff from grain (by blowing wind or air)

winter ~ spend winter

wipeth ~ wipes ~ 2

wise ~ in this way

wist ~ *Arc* knew

wit ~ *Arc* know or learn

wit ~ know ~ 3-

with one accord ~ in agreement or harmony; with one mind; "one-mindedly"; *Gk* one-minded

with ~ *Gk* together with meanwhile

withal ~ *Arc* with; with it, with that, therewith; meanwhile

withdrawest ~ withdraw ~ 1

withdraweth ~ withdraws ~ 1

withereth ~ withers ~ 8

withes ~ pl of withe--tough, flexible twigs used for binding

withheldest ~ withheld ~ 1
withholden ~ withheld
withholdeth ~ restrains
withholdeth ~ withholds ~ 4
within ~ inside
within ~ kjv margin: among
without life ~ *Gk* lifeless
without ~ outside; out-of-doors; *Rare* beyond
withs ~ withes ~ 3
withstand ~ resist, oppose
withstood ~ resisted, opposed
witnesseth ~ witnesses ~ 2
wittingly ~ knowingly
woe worth ~ alas
womankind ~ women in general
wonder ~ sign, miracle
wonderful ~ wonderfully
wonders ~ signs, miracles
wont ~ accustomed
woof ~ weaving term: weft--the yarns carried by the shuttle back and forth across the warp in weaving
worketh ~ works: does; *Gk* works out, produces
worlds ~ *Gk* universe, ages
wormwood ~ bitter-oil yielding plant
worship ~ *Arc* honor, dignity, worthiness
worshippeth ~ worships ~ 6
worthies ~ persons of great worth
wot ~ *Arc* know
wotteth ~ wots: *Arc* knows
would have ~ *Gk* wanted to
would ~ willed, wished, wanted; wanted to, wished to
would ~ will or want; i.e. want or wish that; want to or wish to
would thou wert ~ wish you were
wouldest ~ wanted or wished
wouldest ~ would: will or wish

wound ~ wrapped
woundedst ~ wounded ~ 1
woundeth ~ wounds ~ 1
wreathen ~ coiled, entwined, twisted to form a wreath
wrest ~ twist; distort or change the true meaning, purpose, use, etc.; pervert
writest ~ write ~ 2
writeth ~ writes ~ 1
wrongeth ~ wrongs ~ 1
wroth ~ angry, wrathful, incensed
wrough ~ worked, fashioned; toiled
wrought ~ worked: i.e. boiled, bubbled
wroughtest ~ wrought: worked
ye ~ YOU (plural) ~ 3985-
yea ~ yes
yesternight ~ *Arc* last night, (on) the night before
yet ~ still
yieldeth ~ yields ~ 4
yokefellow ~ companion, partner, associate
yonder ~ over there; at or in that place; i.e. that
you ~ YOU (plural) ~ 2615-
you-ward ~ *Arc* toward YOU (plural) ~ 3
your ~ YOUR (plural) ~ 1776-
yours ~ YOURS (plural) ~ 12-
yourselves ~ YOURSELVES (plural) ~ 191
Zacharias ~ Zachariah ~ 11

Order Blank (p. 2)

Name:____

Address:____

City & State:___________________________Zip:__________

Credit Card #:___________________Expires:________

Other Materials on the KJB & T.R.

[ ] Send *The Last 12 Verses of Mark* by Dean Burgon ($15+$4 S&H) A hardback book 400 pages.

[ ] Send *The Traditional Text* hardback by Burgon ($16 + $4 S&H) A hardback book, 384 pages in length.

[ ] Send *Summary of Traditional Text* by Dr. Waite ($3 +$2)

[ ] Send *Summary of Causes of Corruption*, DAW ($3+$2)

[ ] Send *Causes of Corruption* by Burgon ($15 + $4 S&H) A hardback book, 360 pages in length.

[ ] Send *Inspiration and Interpretation*, Dean Burgon ($25+$4 S&H) A hardback book, 610 pages in length.

[ ] Send *Summary of Inspiration* by Dr. Waite ($3 + $2 S&H)

[ ]Send *Contemporary Eng. Version Exposed*, DAW ($3+$2)

[ ] Send *Westcott & Hort's Greek Text & Theory Refuted by Burgon's Revision Revised--Summarized* by Dr. D. A. Waite ($7.00 + $3 S&H), 120 pages, perfect bound.

[ ] Send *Defending the King James Bible* by Dr.Waite $13+$4 S&H) A hardback book, indexed with study questions.

[ ] Send *Guide to Textual Criticism* by Edward Miller ($7 +$4)

[ ] Send *Westcott's Denial of Resurrection*, Dr. Waite ($4+$3)

[ ] Send *Four Reasons for Defending KJB* by DAW ($3+$3)

[ ] Send *Vindicating Mark 16:9-20* by Dr. Waite ($3+$3 S&H)

[ ] Send *Dean Burgon's Confidence in KJB* by DAW ($3+$3)

[ ] Send *Readability of A.V. (KJB)* by D. A. Waite, Jr. ($6 +$3)

[ ] Send *NIV Inclusive Language Exposed* by DAW ($5+$3)

[ ] Send *26 Hours of KJB Seminar* (4 videos) by DAW ($50.00)

Send or Call Orders to:
THE BIBLE FOR TODAY
900 Park Ave., Collingswood, NJ 08108
Phone: 856-854-4452; FAX:--2464; Orders: 1-800 JOHN 10:9
E-Mail Orders: BFT@BibleForToday.org; Credit Cards OK